NB

KU-027-603

DCPL00003404✦2

941.92

should be returned on or b
n below. Items not alread⁄ ⸝
wers may ⸗ renewed in   ⸗u⸗·ty *Tipperary*
one. To ⸗   w, please ⸗⸗⸗
de label.   ⸗new onl⸗n
an be re⸗   ⸗d at y⸗o⸗⸗ ⸗
᾽ online   ᾽v.du⸗⸗ ⸗
harge⸗   ᾽   rdue⸗ ⸗⸗⸗ ᾽
d in r⸗   am⸗⸗
᾽ed   ᾽€ ᾽

ar⸗⸗

Withdrawn from Stock
Dublin City Public Libraries

Maynooth Studies in Local History

SERIES EDITOR Raymond Gillespie

This volume is one of six short books published in the Maynooth Studies in Local History series in 2010. Like over 85 of their predecessors they range widely over the local experience in the Irish past. That local experience is presented in the complex social world of which it is part, from the world of the dispossessed Irish in 17th-century Donegal to political events in 1830s Carlow; from the luxury of the early 19th-century Dublin middle class to the poverty of the Famine in Tipperary; and from the political activists in Kimmage in 1916 to those who suffered in a different sort of war as their homes were bombed in South Circular Road in 1941. These local experiences cannot be a simple chronicling of events relating to an area within adminis-trative or geographically determined boundaries since understanding the local world presents much more complex challenges for the historian. It is a reconstruction of the socially diverse worlds of poor and rich as well as those who took very different positions on the political issues that preoccupied the local societies of Ireland. Reconstructing such diverse local worlds relies on understanding of what the people of the different communities that made up the localities of Ireland had in common and what drove them apart. Understanding the assumptions, often unspoken, around which these local societies operated is the key to recreating the world of the Irish past and reconstructing the way in which those who inhabited those worlds lived their daily lives. As such, studies such as those presented in these short books, together with their predecessors, are at the forefront of Irish historical research and represent some of the most innovative and exciting work being undertaken in Irish history today. They also provide models which others can follow up and adapt in their own studies of the Irish past. In such ways will we understand better the regional diversity of Ireland and the social and cultural basis for that diversity. If they also convey something of the vibrancy and excitement of the world of Irish local history today they will have achieved at least some of their purpose.

Maynooth Studies in Local History: Number 89

The Famine clearance in Toomevara, County Tipperary

Helen O'Brien

FOUR COURTS PRESS

Set in 10pt on 12pt Bembo by
Carrigboy Typesetting Services for
FOUR COURTS PRESS LTD
7 Malpas Street, Dublin 8, Ireland
www.fourcourtspress.ie
and in North America for
FOUR COURTS PRESS
c/o ISBS, 920 N.E. 58th Avenue, Suite 300, Portland, OR 97213.

© Helen O'Brien and Four Courts Press 2010

ISBN 978–1–84682–260–5

All rights reserved. Without limiting the rights
under copyright reserved alone, no part of this
publication may be reproduced, stored in or intro-
duced into a retrieval system, or transmitted, in any
form or by any means (electronic, mechanical,
photocopying, recording or otherwise), without the
prior written permission of both the copyright
owner and the above publisher of this book.

Printed in Scotland by
Thomson Litho, Glasgow.

Contents

Acknowledgments

I should like to take this opportunity to thank all those who have helped in the research and writing of this study, particularly Professor Ray Gillespie and Dr Terence Dooley of NUI Maynooth who provided invaluable assistance and support.

Throughout the course of the study, several institutions and individuals provided resources, information and help. I would like to thank the Local Studies Library in Thurles, County Tipperary, John Paul II Library NUI Maynooth, the National Library, Nenagh Guardian Ltd, Ordnance Survey Ireland, the National Archives of Ireland and the Director of the National Archives of Ireland. A special thanks to Ms Helena Kilmartin for allowing access to her grandfather's precious memoirs and thanks to Doctor Denis Marnane for his helpful advice and support throughout my studies.

I am very grateful to my family for their support and encouragement and in particular my father, for his inspiring interest in local history. My greatest thanks and appreciation to my husband Kieran, whose patience, love and encouragement made this study possible.

Finally, I would like to dedicate this study to the memory of a wonderful lady, my mother.

Introduction

'When my mind goes back to these years, as I pen these lines, I scarcely can do so as my eyes fill and my heart beats at the recollection'.[1] These words, taken directly from an actual eyewitness account of the Famine in the parish of Toomevara, Co. Tipperary evoke poignant images and stir strong emotions. The Great Famine of 1845–51 irrevocably changed the course of Irish history and had a dramatic impact on countless villages and parishes across the country. The parish of Toomevara in North Tipperary was one such parish, and this study aims to examine the experience of the parish, with particular focus on the clearance which occurred there in 1849.

The Roman Catholic parish of Toomevara is situated in North Tipperary in the barony of Upper Ormond. It encompasses 25,459 acres and is comprised of the earlier civil parishes of Aghnameadle, Ballymackey, Kilkeary, Templedowney and part of the civil parish of Latteragh[2] (figure 1). While the clearance has been briefly mentioned in some local studies, there has not been any study on the Famine in Toomevara, which is surprising given the extent of the clearance and the controversy that ensued.[3] The clearance was so notorious that it became the subject of a parliamentary debate in the house of commons led by the MP for Tipperary, Scully.[4] The study is structured to provide a chronological account of the Famine where possible, with the first chapter focusing on Toomevara prior to the Famine. The second chapter discusses Toomevara's experience of the Famine up until 1849 whereupon the third chapter details the clearance and the event which came to be known locally as the 'hut tumbling'. The fourth chapter focuses on the consequences of the clearance and discusses the overall effect of the Famine on the parish.

In recent years the Great Famine has attracted much scholarly attention and a plethora of works on the topic have been produced.[5] However ample room exists for more local studies on the topic. Local studies have the ability to uncover information that has not been previously examined and it is among these that this study aims to take its place by telling the story of Toomevara during the Famine. Local sources for the study of the Famine can sometimes be difficult to locate. However, in regard to this study, this author was fortunate to have access to the personal memoirs of a local school master Thomas Treacy who was born in 1832 in Toomevara and lived through the Famine (figure 2). His memoirs provide a clear and stark account of the events that occurred there. This type of primary source has been described as the 'most useful qualitative historical source available' as it conveys the experiences of people

1 Location of Toomevara Roman Catholic Parish, Co. Tipperary

living through the particular event.[6] One has to bear in mind though that the recorder is conveying their own interpretation of events and either wittingly or unwittingly conveying their own attitudes, values and beliefs.[7] As long as one is aware of this, a source as rare and important as this can be mined for some invaluable historical information. Folklore sources have also been used in this study. While they are subject to the same bias as the memoir, they portray the general collective social memory of the Famine which has survived in the parish to this day. Balance to the potential bias of the memoir and folklore is provided by reports from local newspapers at the time.

Two local newspapers, the *Nenagh Guardian* and the *Tipperary Vindicator* have proved essential in building a picture of life in Toomevara and the surrounding areas and detailing events which occurred during the Famine. The *Nenagh Guardian* which was first published in Nenagh in 1838 was a conservative Protestant newspaper. The *Tipperary Vindicator* which adopted a much more Catholic nationalist approach ran between 1844 and 1849.[8] The *General valuation of rateable property in Ireland* overseen by Richard Griffith and produced for Toomevara provides more valuable information on housing and land structures in Toomevara towards the end of the Famine.[9]

2 Sample of Thomas Treacy's memoirs

Numerous other primary sources have all helped to complete the study including census reports from the early and mid-19th century, parish baptismal and marriage records, poor law union minute books, and house of commons parliamentary reports.[10] Various letters sent during the early years of the Famine from the locality of Toomevara to the Temporary Relief Commission and now housed in the National Archives provide information on the state of area.[11] Surviving rental records from the Massy Dawson and Cole Bowen estates have provided some insights into the condition of the area prior to and during the early years of the Famine.[12] These were augmented by evidence collected by the the the Poor Inquiry in 1835.[13]

1. Toomevara before the Famine

Toomevara is an area with a rich historical heritage with five ruined castles spread throughout, signifying the importance of the parish in earlier times. These were once the homes of the MacEgan, O'Meara, McGrath and O'Kennedy families. The area was once known as Templedowney. In Toomevara village itself, there are two ancient ecclesiastical ruins. There is some debate as to their origins. It is generally agreed that the site situated in the triangle that serves as the village square belonged to the early Irish religious settlements. However, one source attributes it to the monks of St Odran of the nearby Latteragh monastery.[1] Another source attributes its foundation to a priest, Donan of the Canons of St Augustine in the 7th century. The second ruin was of a later style and is thought to be an Augustinian priory of the Canons Regular but it is open to debate if it was a cell of the Tyone abbey in Nenagh or Mona Incha in Roscrea. However, a grave stone memorial dated to the 1600s in the graveyard declares that Thady O'Meara who is buried on the site was the last prior of Tyone abbey.[2] This would support the claim that it was indeed linked to Tyone abbey. In 1837, the village of Toomevara was described as having 790 inhabitants, a constabulary police station, a national school, a dispensary and four fairs annually mainly for the sale of cattle, corn and butter.[3] Maps of Toomevara in 1840 show that the village was quite extensive (Appendix A).[4]

POPULATION

In the first half of the 19th century, Toomevara parish's population was increasing steadily, mirroring what was happening at a national level. The population figures available prior to 1841 are for civil parishes and not individual townlands, so for comparison purposes the figures below for Latteragh in 1841 include the entire civil parish of Latteragh, rather than its individual townlands that form part of Toomevara Roman Catholic parish.

Table 1.1 shows a steady population increase in each civil parish with a total increase of 18% in the population between 1821 and 1841. This trend is reflective of what was happening within the barony and county which had population increases of 14% and 20% respectively in the same period. From

Leabharlanna Poiblí Chathair Bhaile Átha Cliath
Dublin City Public Libraries

Table 1.1. Population growth in Toomevara, 1821–41[5]

Population Growth, 1821–41

Area	Size (nearest acre)	1821 (pop)	1831 (pop)	1841 (pop)
Aghnameadle	10,322	2,947	3,577	3,893
Ballymackey	9,713	2,980	3,066	3,178
Kilkeary	2,726	453	662	784
Templedowney	1,839	436	475	552
Latteragh	4,065	968	995	1,132
Total	28,665	7,784	8,775	9,539
Upper Ormond	79,471	22,851	24,807	26,530
Tipperary	1,961,722	346,896	402,363	435,553

1841 onwards, it is possible to examine the population figures for individual townlands. Apart from Toomevara village which contained 885 people in 1841, the five townlands with the highest population in the parish show no particular trend in terms of their size. However, of the five most populous townlands, four of them were in areas that had reasonably good quality land such as Ballymackey and Kilkeary. Annual Catholic baptism rates in the parish at this time reflected the general population growth increasing from 212 baptisms in 1840 to 350 in 1845.[6]

HOUSING

The general quality and standard of housing in Toomevara in 1841 appears to have been substantially poorer than throughout the barony or county. There were 1,514 houses in 1841 and over 55% of these were categorized as fourth class.[7] Houses that fell into the fourth-class category were generally one roomed huts made from mud with no windows, typical of the residences of the poorest of the poor in pre-Famine Ireland.

Table 1.2 highlights that the situation varied between civil parishes with some recording lower percentages of fourth-class housing than others. Toomevara village had by far the highest percentage of first-class houses with 4.5% or seven houses in total. However this is not surprising as the village was where the priests, the Church of Ireland minister, the doctor and local land agent for the Massy Dawson estate lived. Ballymackey had the next highest percentage of first-class houses at 2.6%. Ballymackey had the best quality land

Table 1.2. House classifications, 1841[8]

House classifications: 1841 Census

	1st (%)	2nd (%)	3rd (%)	4th (%)
Aghnameadle Rural	0.4	14.3	30.5	54.8
Aghnameadle (Toomevara Village)	4.5	21.8	37.2	36.5
Ballymackey	2.6	9.1	25.1	63.2
Kilkeary	1.6	17.6	38.4	42.4
Templedowney	2.1	10.3	16.5	71.1
Latteragh	0.0	20.0	33.3	46.7
Toomevara Total	1.8	13.8	29.3	55.1
Tipperary	1.5	17.5	44.0	37.0
Lower Ormond	3.2	19.9	41.2	35.6
Upper Ormond	1.4	14.7	36.7	47.1

in the parish and it is not surprising that most of the local landed gentry resided there. However, it also had the second highest percentage of fourth-class housing highlighting the vast gaps between housing standards even within a small area. When looking at Tipperary as a whole, other commentators have remarked that labourers in Tipperary were not as badly off as their counterparts in other counties; the percentage of fourth-class houses recorded for other counties such as Clare was 50% and 58% for both Kerry and Mayo.[9] However, Toomevara it seems was on a par with these counties rather than Tipperary.

LIVING CONDITIONS

Given that there were over 1,500 houses in Toomevara in 1841 and over 1,200 of these were third and fourth-class houses, it is presumed that the vast majority of the people in the area were of the impoverished labouring class.[10] The local doctor Dr Charles Bourns painted a very bleak picture of their living conditions in the 1830s.

> Speaking of the labouring classes, clothes scanty, food dry potatoes, those even scarce in summer. In general, bedding most miserable, dirty and deficient; the common covering consists of the day clothes; furniture, a pot, an apology for a table, a stool and two sticks fastened in the wall as a bedstead. Ventilation studiously avoided; comforts not even thought of.[11]

Those of means in the locality such as the landed gentry, large farmers and large merchants led a very different lifestyle. Advertisements in a local paper for a wide range of luxury products in July 1844 were obviously aimed at this sector of society and highlighted the divergence in living standards. Another article appeared in the same paper informing the public that 'a splendid picnic affair is to come off on Friday, the 9th inst., at, or near Dromineer, which will be composed of the elite of the neighbourhood'.[12]

There is no doubt that alcohol was of huge importance and the centre of all social activities. Dr Bourns said that 'it appears to be the general rule not to leave the towns, markets or fairs sober, Sundays more especially; the great number of public-houses, all open on Sundays, much facilitate the habit'.[13] He remarked that 'the district is generally healthy; it has however, been visited with cholera, and at present has many cases of the common cholera and bowel complaints, induced by the wet, close weather'.[14]

EDUCATION

The level of illiteracy in Toomevara in 1841 was comparable to levels for Tipperary as a whole. Tipperary at the time had the lowest rate of illiteracy in Munster with 51% of people aged five and upwards illiterate. Of those aged five years and upwards in the five civil parishes, a total of 25.2% (2,074 people) were literate.[15] Of the remaining population 22% (1813 people) could read only and 52.8% (4,349 people) were illiterate. Thomas Treacy's grandfather Andrew Tierney was employed as a school teacher in Toomevara in the very early years of the 19th century.[16] He was given a house and three acres of land in Baynanagh for teaching 'any orphaned in the estate of Mr Dawson at Toomevara'. Educational provisions improved significantly in the 25-year-period prior to the Famine mainly due to the establishment of the first national schools in 1831. In 1821, there were two locally funded all boy schools in the parish. By 1841, this had increased to three schools, two of which catered for girls.[17] By 1841, there were 334 children attending these schools, a fourfold increase on the attendance in 1821.[18]

From 1830 to 1845, 15 Catholic churches were built across north-west Tipperary.[19] Worth noting is that no fewer than three of these were built in Toomevara which would have meant that a significant amount of money was collected from the parish to help fund the buildings. Grennanstown chapel which was built on the site of an earlier one was substantially subscribed to by Count Peter Dalton who was high sheriff for Tipperary in 1839.[20] The other two chapels which were built at considerable cost to the parish were located in Gortagarry and Ballinree and were completed in the early 1840s.[21] Thus, despite the high levels of poverty, the Catholic church could still manage to collect sufficient funds to facilitate this.

OCCUPATIONS

In 1841 72.9% of families in the parish were employed in agriculture and 10.5% in manufacturing or trade. A further 16.6% of families recorded their occupation as 'other pursuits'.[22] This was similar to the percentages recorded for the barony of Upper Ormond thus emphasizing the strong dependence on agriculture as a means of livelihood. However, at this time, a local solicitor ominously remarked that the labouring class were in need of assistance as there was 'not labour enough for them'.[23] There were a small number of other job opportunities available in the area. A large public contractor employed over 50 men daily in 1845.[24] The general rate of wages per day in the district was around 8*d*.[25] Milling appeared to be quite prominent within the immediate area of Toomevara. Of 50 mills spread across Upper Ormond, Lower Ormond and Owney and Arra, five were located in Toomevara alone at Ollatrim, Ballyknockane, Ballymackey and Garrane.[26] Smaller numbers were employed in alternative sectors such as clothing, lodging, furniture, machinery, health, transport, education etc.[27] However, on the eve of the Famine in Toomevara, employment for the most part was dependent on agriculture.

AGRICULTURE

Size of holdings
Of the 3,164 agricultural holdings throughout Upper Ormond in 1841, 60% contained less than 15 acres.[28] John Kennedy, a former shop keeper and land holder in Nenagh, estimated that without doing extra labouring work, four acres would be the minimum amount of land needed to support a family.[29] This would suggest that close to 34% of holdings in Upper Ormond were considered too small to support families without extra income. While holdings of varying sizes existed in each area, O'Brien Dillon of Laurel Lodge, Nenagh, solicitor for the Massy Dawson estate in Toomevara and a landed proprietor himself estimated that the usual size of holdings around the Nenagh area was 'from 15 to 20 acres'. Adam Walker, a magistrate and land agent who lived in Nenagh estimated that the usual size of farms in the district was smaller than this, mainly 'from five to 10 acres and 15; a few from 20 to 50: very few above that'.[30]

Landowners
The General Valuation of 1850 showed that most of the land in the parish was owned by a small number of landowners who lived in other areas of the country or in England. While the ownership of many estates changed hands after the Famine, there is no evidence to show that the landowners in

Toomevara had sold any of their land by 1850. Robert Cole Bowen of Bowenscourt, Co. Cork owned land which extended throughout Ballymackey and part of Templedowney. Mrs Otway Cave of the nearby Otway Estate in Templederry owned over 1,000 acres in Aghnameadle and Latteragh. George Fawcett, one of the largest land owners in the area had extensive lands throughout Aghnameadle. The Otway Caves and Count D'Alton were the only ones who had residences in close vicinity to Toomevara and they usually spent some of the year at these residences. Count D'Alton of Grenanstown House, a Catholic, owned over one thousand acres in Kilkeary and Ballymackey. The Honourable O.F.G. Toler owned over 2,000 acres in Ballymackey and Kilkeary.[31]

The Revd Massy Dawson of Ballynacourty in the Glen of Aherlow, South Tipperary owned less than 2,000 acres of land in the parish of Toomevara.[32] The vast majority of his estate was in the Glen of Aherlow in South Tipperary and the remainder was divided between the baronies of Eliogarty, Middlethird and Iffa and Offa West making him one of the largest land owners in the county.[33] While Massy Dawson was not the largest land owner in the parish in 1840, he owned the entire village of Toomevara which contained the bulk of the parish's population. He also held land and properties in 12 townlands with 98 families of tenants in total.[34] The few rental records that have survived highlight the increasing arrears that the tenants in Toomevara were accumulating in the decade prior to the Famine.[35] From 1833, the amount of arrears increased from £1,310 to £2,496 in 1842. On the Cole Bowen estate in Ballymackey, the situation was replicated. Between 1839 and 1843, arrears increased fourfold.[36] It is evident therefore that many of those living in Toomevara were unable to pay their rent and were declining further into poverty ever before the potato blight struck.

Agricultural practices and conflict

Almost all of those interviewed at the Nenagh session of the Devon Commission who were acquainted with agricultural practices in the area agreed that agricultural practices had improved.[37] Subletting and subdivision of land were still prevalent in some areas but efforts were being made to stop these practices. However, efforts to consolidate holdings 'to get rid of the pauper tenantry' appear to have caused considerable agrarian unrest. J.A. Braddell recalled only one instance of farm consolidation on the Cole Bowen estate in Ballymackey.[38] After the consolidation the new lessee and his caretakers were the victims of outrages.[39]

The land in Toomevara appears to have been mainly used for tillage farming and the 'usual rent for average good land' in the area was about '40s. the acre'.[40] In north-west Tipperary, leases in general were scarce before the Famine, although the situation varied from estate to estate.[41] O'Brien Dillon commented on the situation locally. Leases were generally held from year to year in Toomevara; the 'conacre' system prevailed and labourers paid from 50s. to £3 for a house and garden which they chiefly earned by rearing and selling a pig. Labourers' wages were generally paid in cash by the farmers throughout the district but sometimes in potatoes.[42]

O'Brien Dillon remarked that the number of agrarian outrages had increased considerably between 1840 and 1845 and he attributed this to the increase in evictions that had occurred in this period. When asked if allowing arrears to accumulate led to eviction of tenants, O'Brien Dillon said 'On the estate that I am connected with, Mr Massy Dawson's, I think the tenants have been injured by indulgence'. He remarked that this accumulation of arrears had not been allowed due to neglect or indulgence but 'from mistaken benevolence'. He named Massy Dawson as one of three landlords within the locality who gave assistance to tenants and made 'very liberal allowances'. His evidence, however, would have to be judged bearing his occupation in mind.

Middlemen appear to have been present in most areas and were disliked by all. O'Brien Dillon said 'the anxiety is to hold under the head landlord and get rid of the middlemen'. Most of Toomevara village was held under middlemen.[43] John A. Braddell, agent for the Cole Bowen estate commented on the situation in Ballymackey complaining that while the greater portion of the land was occupied by direct lessees on the estate, where land was held under middlemen, the under-tenants were subject to much harsher treatment and higher rent. Whereas a landlord found it very difficult to find a tenant for a holding from which a tenant had been evicted: 'a middleman was often able to get friends of his'. Any consequential outrages 'would depend on local circumstances'.[44]

Crime and sources of conflict

Pre Famine Tipperary was notorious for its high level of crime. In 1841, it was said 'In no district, shire or county in the kingdom is there more crime perpetrated with impunity than in this far-famed and celebrated county'.[45] The most common outrages in Upper Ormond from 1837 to 1841 were threatening notices, assault, house attacks and incendiarism.[46] The majority of the violence appears to have been related to agrarian issues. Crime was so prevalent that on 5 June 1836 a branch of The Tipperary Society for the Prevention of Outrage and Maintenance of the Peace was formed in eight parishes in Tipperary including Toomevara.[47] It was noted in a local newspaper that these parishes were the ones with high incidences of agrarian crimes and faction riots.

In the year to August 1845, there were 24 cases of crime in the parish of Toomevara reported in the local newspaper.[48] Seven of these were assault, nine were cases where threatening notices were posted and at four of these shots were fired. There were also three cases of shootings, three cases of incendiarism, a case of stolen arms and lastly a case where a raid was carried out and arms were recovered. Patrick Kennedy of Cloncannon died after being assaulted during a faction fight. Edmond Gleeson in Latteragh was assaulted and died from his injuries. Most of the threatening notices and gun shots were directed at men who had either leased land which had become available due to tenant eviction or had evicted tenants themselves. Patrick Hogan of Glenaguile's house was broken into and a group served a threatening notice on him to give up a couple of acres which had recently been dispossessed from another person. A party of men entered Thomas Kelly's house at Monanore and assaulted him in May 1845. It was reported that in December 1845 a large party of Terry Alt boys went to the residence of Revd Mr Studdart at Ballymackey and posted a threatening notice.[49] The group shouted for Mr Studdart to come out but they did not break into the house. The 'Terry Alts' and 'Rockites' were among many secret societies founded in Ireland from the 18th century onwards which were involved in agrarian agitation in pre-Famine Ireland.[50]

John A. Braddell said there were 'a great number' of agrarian outrages in the time that he had been a land agent in North Tipperary and that these 'were all about the turning out from land, and new tenants coming in'.[51] He recalled one case in the late 1830s where a man who was put in as caretaker to an evicted holding was murdered. Revd M. O'Connor, a curate in Roscrea in 1844 and previously a curate in Scariff and Toomevara attributed the cause of this murder to the eviction of 'industrious and independent' Catholic tenants in favour of Protestant tenants. This action by Cole Bowen caused outrage among the tenants and so 'unfortunate blood letting' followed.[52] It was obviously felt at certain levels that there was an unusually high disturbance rate in Toomevara. After describing the poor people of Roscrea as 'very docile and good, if they had some encouragement – if they had the means of living', Revd Michael O'Connor explained the difference in behaviour between the people of Roscrea and Toomevara by saying:

The people of Toomevara are the descendants of the old ancient families, who had large tracts of land, and whose families were connected throughout the country. Here was an uncle, and you go thirty miles and find a nephew, all very comfortable and independent; when one party was affected, it would vibrate through up through the whole, and go through the whole: that excitement would be begun there and be kept up through the whole district.[53]

From this response, it would appear that there was a strong bond amongst some of the people of the parish.

Another common feature of life at the time in Toomevara were faction fights, popular in Tipperary as a whole; indeed it was regarded as the county where faction fighting originated. A faction fight was described as 'in essence, a trial of strength between families, clans, namesakes, baronies or parishes, the remote cause of the fight being, perhaps, some insult, real or imaginary, on one side or the other'.[54] Thomas Treacy recalled numerous factions in the area who traditionally opposed each other, the 'two years olds' and the 'three years olds' and the 'white feet' and 'black feet'. The nickname 'black feet' is attributed to one family in Toomevara to the present day. He remarked that 'Every locality had its own members of a faction and this spread until a faction would perhaps number one thousand men spread over localities, parishes, baronies and even counties'. It seems it was not uncommon for family members to take opposing sides. 'These party fights were wholly outside consanguinity as very near relatives were opposed to each other'. 'They met at the next fair, dance, hurling and prepared for active conflict, each member came armed with a short stick, chiefly blackthorn about three feet long'. Thomas Treacy recalled a specific fight he witnessed;

> I have seen a faction fight of two hundred men at each side, the poor fools were drawn up opposite each other, perhaps about one hundred yards asunder and at a signal from the heads rushed to meet, though it was melancholy to witness the scene, it was laughingly enjoyed by neutrals and members of the government, such flying of sticks, cracking of heads, shouts and huzzas, much resembling an Indian meeting of foes. It was usual for the heads to ply their followers with an amount of bad whiskey; the combat was continued till one party gave way.[55]

It seems that local police were not inclined to make genuine efforts to stop or prevent these faction fights. Treacy remarked that;

> The would be law protectors, 'Peelers' were drafted into the village fair green, but only as glorified spectators. They were sure to keep out of the way, see the beginning, climax and end, then might make a few arrests, lodge them in the barracks for a few hours, liberate them and all was over.[56]

In the early 19th century kinship among people seemed the most important thing when it came to facing your enemies; Thomas Treacy commented that 'it was not how much money you have, but the number you could count on as a connection'.[57]

EMIGRATION

Given the socio-economic climate of the time, it was inevitable that emigration would become a choice for many. Evidence from the Poor Inquiry suggests that emigration from north-west Tipperary was quite low in the 1830s.[58] However, this seems to have changed by the 1840s. In 1844, O'Brien Dillon remarked that there was 'great emigration from this district'.[59] The emigrants were 'rather a decent respectable class of persons, with moderate means' and mainly went to Canada and the United States. It was reported in the local paper that on one particular day in mid-April 1844, the streets of Nenagh were crowded with the number of country people who were leaving to emigrate to America. An advertisement on behalf of a Cork emigration agent, John Besnard appeared in *The Guardian* in September inviting applications for free emigration to Sydney.[60] Thomas Treacy makes reference to his aunt and uncle who emigrated to Canada from the parish in 1845.[61]

Overall, the situation in Toomevara parish on the eve of the Famine was pretty bleak. The population had been increasing steadily since 1821, the housing standard was very poor with over half of the houses classified as nothing more than one roomed huts. Living conditions were appalling for the labouring class. Tipperary had a very high rate of crime and Toomevara was recognized as a parish where it was particularly prevalent. Massy Dawson may have been considered by some to be overly benevolent towards his tenants, but it seems that there were a number of middlemen on his estate. While money may have been raised for the building of three new chapels, rental arrears had been increasing at such a rate on the Massy Dawson estate in Toomevara that they almost doubled between 1833 and 1842. On the Cole Bowen estate in Ballymackey, arrears had increased fourfold in the space of four years. The vast majority of people were dependent on agriculture as the main source of employment. Any further dislocation of the agrarian economy would have fatal consequences. This is precisely what happened in the years after 1845.

2. Famine, 1845–9

The first report in relation to the appearance of blight locally was published in mid-October 1845 in a local newspaper.[1] The crop failure was the worst failure for over a century.[2] Throughout the poor law union of Nenagh, the extent of the damage varied between localities with some areas escaping relatively lightly while others were badly affected.[3] It is estimated that one quarter to one third of the potato crop of 1845 was ruined.[4] This spelled disaster for the poorest of society who were dependent on the potato for their staple food. In Toomevara, Thomas Tracey wrote that

> this year the potatoes, the chief food of the poorer classes blackened, that is about July the stalks were blasted, the leaves withered and when the tubers were being dug they were found to be partly of black hard patches, quite useless as a food. I saw them grated by the poor people and sought to be made into potato bread, no use they could not sustain life, disease set in.[5]

In response to the crisis, a national Relief Commission was established in November 1845 and it in turn directed that local relief committees were to be set up.[6] The Board of Works undertook schemes to employ people so that they would be able to purchase provisions until the following year's crop was harvested.[7]

By early 1846 22 local relief committees were set up in Nenagh poor law union.[8] Almost all of Toomevara parish was under the administration of the Ballymackey relief committee and the Toomevara relief committee.[9] However, 3,336 acres of the parish containing 1,006 people fell within the administration of two other committees.[10] The civil parish of Kilkeary fell under the Ballinclough and Kilkeary committee and two townlands fell under the Templederry and Latteragh committee. Almost 70% of the relief committees' districts were based on Church of Ireland parishes, reflecting the strong influence of Church of Ireland members.[11]

The local committees raised substantial amounts for the relief of hardship. The government gave a donation to each committee based on the amount raised locally. An analysis of eight relief committees in the Nenagh Union, which included Ballymackey committee and Ballinclough and Kilkeary committee showed that 69% of subscriptions were from the gentry, 16% from farmers and merchants, 14% from clergy and 3% from others.[13]

Table 2.1. Religious composition of local relief committees[12]

Committee	Total members	Catholics	Protestants
Ballymackey	11	3	8
Toomevara	10	6	4
Templederry & Latteragh	10	7	3
Ballinaclough & Kilkeary	15	9	6

There were 21 subscribers to the Ballymackey relief fund between April and August 1846. The main subscribers were Major Jackson, a local landowner who donated £15 and Revd John Meagher P.P. who gave £10.[14] By 1850, Major Jackson owned and leased a modest 196 acres in Toomevara which he sublet to tenants.[15] Peter Smithwick, who owned land at Wilton and Shanbally in Ballymackey gave £7.[16] James Willington and James J. Willington of Castle Willington, Ballymackey donated £5 each.[17] They held land in Ballymackey, Aghnameadle and Kilkeary. The Cole Bowen estate which owned thousands of acres in Toomevara donated the sum of £30 to the relief fund earlier in the year.[18] There were smaller contributions made by others also.[19] Some of these such as Denis Loughnane and Thomas Lewis were listed as holding farms of 29 acres and 21 acres in 1850.[20] They gave £1 and 3s. 0d. respectively.[21] However, there were many other medium to large sized farmers throughout Ballymackey who were not recorded as having contributed. Table 2.2 shows the amount of local subscriptions and government grants according to relief committee reports in August and September 1846.

Table 2.2. Finances for local relief committees up to September 1846[22]

Committee	Local Subscription	Government Donations
Ballymackey	£75 2s. 6d.	£503
Toomevara	£107 5s. 0d.	£120
Templederry & Latteragh	£116 2s. 6d.	£90
Ballinaclough & Kilkeary	£71 5s. 0d.	£45

The three main relief committees serving Toomevara had commenced selling Indian meal to the poor of the parish by late spring 1846. The numbers depending on this relief increased substantially over the following months with 25% of the district's population being relieved by the end of the summer. Those in the Kilkeary–Ballinaclough district appear to have been in a worse position with 43% of its relief district's population receiving relief. This was quite high compared to other relief districts in the Union.[23]

The Board of Works sanctioned 16 public works for Upper Ormond in 1846 to provide employment for the poor.[24] The public works in the Toomevara area were to include lowering hills between the townslands of Clash and Knockane; road improvement in Ballymackey; lowering two hills near Toomevara; constructing a new road at Gortagarry and a new road joining Gortagarry and Latteragh. These works were in addition to local employment efforts made by the relief committees. By August, Toomevara committee had spent about £54 10s. on providing local employment and £10 on administration and contingency expenses.[25] At the height of the local works in the village, 50 people were employed in white washing houses, making shores throughout the village and in quarrying flags for the shores. In May 1846 a further 85 people were employed in Ballymackey filling in roadside dykes.[26]

Nationally there was much criticism of how the public works operated.[27] Criticisms of the high rate of wages which it was claimed were usually 9d. or 10d. per day but sometimes as much as 1s. were levelled. It was felt that these high wages enticed labourers away from other forms of employment on farms and with private employers. However labourers in Toomevara were only paid between 4d. and 8d. per day.[28] Another criticism levelled was the manner in which individuals were chosen for employment on the schemes of work.[29] The official selection for places on the relief works was not always adhered to in Toomevara. A letter was sent from the Office of Public Works to the committee suggesting that irregularities in the distribution of labour tickets should be checked. Tickets for the public works were authorized by someone from the relief committee. The Board reported that although tickets issued by the committee were authorized by different members the handwriting appeared to belong to only one member. They issued a direction saying that this practice should be stopped. The Toomevara Relief committee requested a further supply of tickets for the labourers working on the new line of road at Gortagarry in July 1846. However the Office of Public Works replied to them 'begging to suggest the propriety' of having a further supply of tickets forwarded.[30]

Nationally, the relief measures put in place by the government for the first year of the Famine were considered to be mostly successful.[31] Relief efforts were due to end in August 1846 when the new potato crop would become available.[32] A high yield of potatoes was essential in the autumn of 1846, if extreme deprivation was to be avoided. However, the local constabulary estimated that the acreage of potatoes planted in the parish had decreased from 1,200 in 1845 to 921 in 1846.[33] The potato crop of 1846 was virtually a total failure.[34] Constabulary reports from Toomevara estimated that only one-third of the crop in the locality had blight in 1846; however it has been suggested that these estimates were lower than the actual blight levels.[35]

Due to the repeated potato failure, the relief committee in Toomevara was reassembled in autumn 1846 with George Garvey as chairman.[36] Garvey was a magistrate from nearby Moneygall and lived at Thornvale on the border of Tipperary and Offaly. He was a landlord himself as well as being an extensive land agent in Co. Offaly. Other members of the committee included Father John Meagher (treasurer); the Revd Robert Going (secretary) and rector of Toomevara; Revd M. Bourke; Revd D. Molony; Benjamin Hawkshaw (local landowner); John Meagher of Ballybeg (local landowner); Morgan O'Brien (poor law guardian for Aghnameadle) and Jeremiah Toohey (owner of Ollatrim mills).[37] The relief committee in Ballymackey reformed on 30 September 1846.[38] James Willington of Castle Willington was proposed as chairman and the committee consisted mainly of clergy, local landowners and large tenant farmers. Members included Fr Meagher P.P., Revd Sutddert and Revd Thomas Joyce, William P. Poe, Peter Smithwick, William Middleton, James J. Willington (secretary), William Jackson (treasurer), Edward Parker, Major Jackson, J. Jackson, Mr Henry Hill and the local poor law guardians of the parish. Large tenant farmers on the committee included Richard Coughlan and Denis Loughnane. Kilkeary was included in the Ballinaclough Kilkeary relief committee, but there were no landowners from Kilkeary on the committee.[39]

At this stage, the situation was deteriorating rapidly for local people. By spring 1846, 66.6% of labourers in the electoral division of both Ballymackey and Aghnameadle were unemployed. This was the fifth-highest level of unemployment throughout the 24 electoral divisions that comprised the poor law union of Nenagh.[40] In September, the parish priest in Toomevara, Fr John Meagher, sent a letter to the Relief Commission complaining that there were no public works in the immediate vicinity and urged that a meal depot be established in Toomevara or Nenagh.[41] He spoke of the 'deplorable condition of the people' of his parish and said that many of them were 'living on cabbages'. The poor would soon have no choice but to 'starve or rob'. Reports began to appear of animals being killed and their carcasses carried away for food throughout the district. This escalated in the following years with a marked increase in the number of thefts of money and food in 1848 and 1849. Quantities of money and food were stolen. These robberies mainly took place at private residences, however Stephen Devany's shop in Toomevara was broken into in April 1849 while the family were asleep overhead and tobacco, teas, sugar, bread and 30 shillings were stolen. In March 1848, Michael Cash and John Kiely of Garnafana, Toomevara stole five sheep from a Boyd of Clash. Boyd had seen them and called the police. Their houses were searched immediately and the police found that the sheep had already been killed and some of the meat was cooking.[42]

The lord lieutenant had ordered public works to be restarted nationally and by September 1846, there were 109 people on public works at Toomevara at a rate of 8*d*. per day.[43] A public meeting was held in September and October in Toomevara school house to discuss applying for a £1,000 loan to fund public works. However the application was not passed by the Board of Works due to demands for compensation made by the landowners whose land would be affected.[44] Works which were eventually sanctioned for the Toomevara area included lowering a hill at Carrigdawson; building a bridge on the road between Toomevara and Martin Hine's house at Monanore and building gullets at Monanore Cross, at James Meara's house at Grawn, at Mr Powell's house at Blean and another on the road from Silvermines to Toomevara.[45] In January 1847, a Road Sessions meeting was held in Nenagh at which these works were tendered for.[46] The following April, totals of £581 and £3,491 were allocated to Ballymackey and Aghnameadle electoral divisions respectively to complete the public works.

For those of means in the parish and wider locality, life continued as normal. In May, the gentry of the Union held a charity ball in the courthouse in Nenagh, the proceeds of which were donated to the poor of the town. Healthy crops of early wheat were reported throughout the Union and later in the month well-publicized plans were afoot for the Lough Derg Yacht Club annual Regatta. Continuous advertisements for luxury household goods appeared locally. Musical concerts were held in the courthouse in September. In October, Nenagh Union Agricultural Society held a dinner in Brundleys hotel in Nenagh where 40 gentlemen sat down to an 'excellent and substantial meal' and drank toasts to the Queen, the Lord Lieutenant, Prince Albert and the rest of the royal family.[47]

Food exports from Ireland continued in 1846. It has been argued that if this food had been kept in Ireland, it would have bridged the 'starvation gap' between the potato failure in 1846 and the arrival of imported maize the following winter.[48] By the time food prices started to decrease in spring 1847, it was too late for many. Their only source of income had been the public works and the money earned there was 'too low to sustain life'.[49] There were instances of abuse reported within the scheme in Toomevara with some not turning up for work, others sending substitutes in their place and some involved in other work, which shows that people not strictly entitled to positions on the public works secured them in place of others who were far more in need.[50]

At the end of January 1847, the government decided that they would end all public works that year. This marked the point at which they washed their hands of the situation in Ireland. The Poor Law guardians were to assume responsibility for relief efforts. In order to facilitate this, the government passed the Poor Law Extension act. As part of the Poor Law Extension act, any person who held more than a quarter of an acre of land was denied relief.[51] This effectively meant that those who had previously survived on small plots now faced a choice between staying in their homes and starving or giving up their holdings in order to become eligible for relief.

Although the potato crop of 1847 was generally healthy, the catastrophe of 1846 had meant that the people, especially the poor had not been able to plant enough potato seed and had no chance of providing for themselves. A local paper reported that 'destitution is daily increasing and employment diminishing. Nearly every electoral division in Nenagh union is over-run with paupers'.[52] Thomas Tracey remarked that in Toomevara 'it was not till '47 that the real climax of Famine came'.[53] By early 1847, the relief committee in Toomevara had raised £120 10s. in subscriptions and the Relief Commission gave a grant of £120 in respect of this.[54] A soup kitchen was set up in Toomevara.[55] However, all soup kitchens were closed in September and after this all relief became the responsibility of the Poor Law unions.[56]

Any able-bodied person in receipt of poor relief was then made work on the public road works.[57] However, while these may have been considered lucky to procure relief, the quality of what they received varied. In July 1847, a report from a Ballymackey relief committee meeting highlighted that the rations which were being given to the poor were crawling with vermin. Revd Evanson remarked that 'it is not the first time Mr Toohey has given vile meal – it is not fit for pigs and I would not give it to my dogs'. The meal which had been supplied by one of the men on the relief committee highlights the way in some of those of means in the area took advantage of the situation to line their own pockets. A new supplier was then found.[58]

By the end of July 1847, the public works throughout Upper Ormond and other baronies in North Tipperary were ending. Under instruction, local relief committees struck all the able bodied people from their relief lists.[59] This left many with the choice of starvation or the workhouse. The workhouse for the union had opened in December 1841 and could accommodate 600 adults and 400 children.[60] In March 1845, 24% of the 356 inmates were from Toomevara highlighting the impoverished state in which they found themselves even before the blight struck. The number of inmates in the workhouse increased from 830 in May 1846 to 1,047 in July the following year.[61] However, while life in the workhouse was very strict and tough, it was acknowledged by visitors that it was generally well run.[62] As conditions worsened throughout the Famine years many people had to resort to the workhouse. Three separate auxiliary workhouses were set up in 1848 and 1849 in Nenagh town to cope with the overflow.[63]

In July 1847 there was a large increase in fever in Nenagh and its vicinity from which hundreds of people died. A local paper reported that 'fever and dysentery are completing the work which Famine and destitution begun'.[64] That month a temporary fever hospital was authorized for Toomevara by the Central Board of Health in 1847. At a meeting to discuss the hospital the agent

Middleton, on behalf of Massy Dawson offered a house on the Pallas road for free due to the urgent need. It was reported that 58 people in the area had fever, three of whom had been compelled to lie in a ditch the previous night. A committee was set up to run the hospital under the chairmanship of Revd Evanson; rector of Toomevara with Michael Meagher, a large tenant farmer, as secretary. After much confusion and dispute, Dr Kittson, the local dispensary doctor was appointed as medical attendant to the fever hospital. Revd Evanson and Middleton had secretly replied to a letter from the Board of Health recommending a doctor from Moneygall, Dr Bindon, for the position of medical attendant. The relief committee knew nothing of this until they received a letter from the board confirming the recommendation of Dr Bindon. The committee sent a letter to the Board of Health protesting against the recommendation of Dr Bindon and instead recommended Dr Kittson, the local dispensary doctor. The Board quashed the original recommendation and appointed Dr Kittson. The following month they advertised for tenders for the supply of bread, oatmeal, tea, sugar, wine, whiskey, beef, new milk, sour milk, candles, soap and coffins for the hospital.[65] Thomas Tracey recalled that the hospital 'gave admittance but only to human skeletons, spent and worn out by diseases and Famine'.[66]

In September 1847, the running of Toomevara and Ballymackey Fever Hospital was transferred from the local committee to the poor law union on the instruction of the government inspector.[67] A finance committee was set up for the district to examine the accounts of the hospital and furnish the guardians with a weekly return of the expenditure.[68] The committee consisted of Revd Evanson, Fr Meagher, James Willington, Peter Smithwick and John Meagher.[69] At this stage, Dr Kittson reported that fever was on the increase in the area and of a worse type than before. There were 80 patients in the fever hospital at that time at a cost of about six pence per patient per day. Yet despite this and the reason is unclear, the Fever Hospital was closed the following April/May 1848 by order of the Central Board of Health. Fr Meagher distributed some of the hospital clothing to the poor of the area which caused some discussion at a board of guardians meeting. The guardians were of the opinion that these should have been given to them. Revd Mr Evanson, rector of Toomevara and chairman of the Relief Committee of Toomevara reported that Fr Meagher had distributed some of the clothing to the poor of the area.[70]

It was recorded at a Nenagh poor law union meeting that the numbers applying for relief in Ballymackey were increasing daily in September 1847.[71] The desperation of some was highlighted when it was reported that a two-year-old heifer belonging to Jeremiah Toohey of Ollatrim was killed on his lands at Clash in June 1847. The carcass was taken and the head, feet and entrails were left behind. On 28 October, an estimated crowd of 200 people from Toomevara and Ballymackey assembled at the gates of the workhouse in

Nenagh demanding outdoor relief.[72] They forced the gates open and called out for the guardians to give them provisions. It was reported that the crowd were: 'manifesting no riotous disposition and whose miserable appearance plainly bespoke the extent of their sufferings which strange to say, they would not mitigate by seeking admission into the house'. They later dispersed on the assurance that a relieving officer appointed for Aghnameadle and Ballymackey would set to work the following morning.

A letter from Michael Hogan was read at the Union meeting on the same day stating that out of a population of 4,000 in the electoral division of Ballymackey and Toomevara, there were almost 1,700 destitute.[73] James Willington confirmed this to be accurate. However, despite their destitution, all those on Michael Hogan's list had objected to coming to the workhouse. Thomas Tracey offered his interpretation as to why this was the case:

> The workhouses were filled from floor to ceilings, and it was such a reproach to be called a 'poor house pauper' that the people suffered starvation and death sooner than enter. If a family say (as hundred of times occurred), young father and mother with a few children entered the workhouse, the husband was separated from the wife, and both from the children, even the loving Irish children were separated from each other according to sex. The wailings of these I hear now … many of whom when they became inmates never saw each other again.[74]

Under the Irish Poor Relief Extension act of 1847, the Nenagh poor law union guardians had to appoint nine relieving officers in the Union who would assess poor relief applicants and oversee the distribution of relief in their area. Timothy O'Brien who was a brother to Morgan O'Brien, guardian for Aghnameadle was elected as relieving officer to Aghnameadle and Ballymackey at a salary of £38 per annum. There was considerable coverage in the local paper that six of the nine relieving officers elected were all relatives of existing guardians of the poor law union.[75] Timothy O'Brien was to attend Toomevara on Mondays, Clash on Tuesdays and Saturdays and Ballymackey on Fridays.[76]

On 11 November, only two weeks after the crowd from Ballymackey and Toomevara had assembled at the workhouse, around 300 people from the same areas gathered once more at the workhouse demanding outdoor relief or employment.[77] It was reported that 'they appeared to be in extreme destitution'. This time they were accompanied by five or six of the farmers who paid the heaviest rates from the area. When they were admitted to the board room, they said that the people were in a state of destitution; they had no food or employment and were starving. Even if they were to starve, they wouldn't go to the workhouse. Perhaps their intentions became clear when they warned that the property of the 'well disposed and peaceable inhabitants of the parish' was not safe as the poor were likely to plunder unless they got outdoor relief. The chairman explained that the law did not allow the guardians to give outdoor relief to the able bodied until the workhouse was full.[78] The crowd dispersed peacefully.

A week later the chairman of the board of guardians R.U. Bayly, was returning home to Ballinaclough with his brother-in-law from his Nenagh office when shots were fired at them.[79] However, it was felt that the attack resulted from Bayly's activities as a land agent and not as a guardian.[80] William Carthy from Ballymackey and another man named Daly from Kilkeary were later hanged for the offence in Clonmel. When arrested, Carthy was found to have £8 10s. on his person which was reported to have been collected by subscription to facilitate his escape to America.[81]

By December 1847 the situation in Toomevara was deplorable. James Willington said at the Board of Guardian meeting: 'I assure you that the people in our district are in an actual state of starvation, at least the greater number of them. They cannot be in a worse state'.[82] While death rates are not available for Toomevara for the early Famine years, the impact on the birth rate was evident. The number of Catholic baptisms decreased from a peak of 350 in 1845 to 274 in 1846, a decrease of 22%. A further decrease was recorded in 1847 resulting in an aggregate decline of 26% in the two years. This was in marked contrast to the steady increase in baptisms in the years leading up to 1845 mentioned in the first chapter.[83]

The Poor Law system itself was unable to deal with the challenges it faced and incompetent administrators only served to worsen the fate of the destitute. In December 1847 James Willington reported that Timothy O'Brien, the relieving officer, had not attended Ballymackey for the previous three Fridays and had only returned the name of one person to be considered for relief. Pat McGrath, another guardian said that 'the people are really starving in the ditches'. James Willington pressed the plight of those in Ballymackey the following week saying 'the destitution and suffering of the poor of Ballymackey is alarming'.[84] O'Brien was dismissed in January 1848 for incompetency.[85] Three other relieving officers were also dismissed the following month. The guardian McGrath said that 'the poor of Ballymackey and other places have been neglected by the relieving officer, namely O'Brien, for instead of giving them relief it was card playing and gambling he used to be employed with'. The chairman, John Bayly commented that it was the guardian's own fault and reminded them of the previous September when they elected many of their own relatives as relieving officers. Ignatius O'Leary, a new relieving officer for Ballymackey and Aghnameadle was appointed in February, 1848.[86]

The frustration felt by many of the guardians was evident at union meetings in 1848. Poor law regulations prevented them from giving relief to many who were destitute. There was very little employment available for the able-bodied destitute and the only alternative for many was the workhouse. Those who were eligible for outdoor relief worked at stone breaking. There were four areas in Toomevara appointed as depots for stone breaking.[87] These included Ballinree quarry and Coolderry in Ballymackey and Kilinafinch and Ballybeg in Aghnameadle. As happened in 1847 the only relief offered was admittance to the workhouse. Testament to the destitution and starvation that the people were suffering at the time was a request sent by the Board of Guardians in December 1847 to the Poor Law Commissioners requesting their permission to give coffins to the destitute that died outside the workhouse. However, this request was refused. Captain Darley, the poor law inspector said 'the time is now come when every exertion should be made to keep the people from starving. The work in the country has ceased – the potato planting has terminated and no employment is to be had'. He also commented on the level of misery in Aghnameadle and said 'it is almost a second Skibbereen'. The board received a sealed order from the Poor Law Commissioners in June in response to an earlier request granting limited outdoor relief to a small number of able bodied people if they were in an utter state of destitution.[88] By July, it was recorded that there were 400 people in the village of Toomevara receiving outdoor relief.[89]

Despite the numbers that were starving, there were numerous reports of outdoor relief being given to those who were not officially entitled to it. Two local guardians by the name of Willington and O'Brien alleged that there were people with several acres of land in Aghnameadle receiving outdoor relief. In April Pat McGrath, guardian for Ballymackey electoral division said he had given money and relief to 'girls and women who wore veils and bonnets' because they were returned for relief by the guardian, John Meagher of Ballybeg. McGrath also said that ratepayers in Kilinafinch had complained to him that there were people who owned cattle receiving relief. Another dispute arose in May when John Meagher of Ballybeg was accused of obtaining meal for the use of the poor but keeping it himself. It was highlighted within the Union that some people in receipt of outdoor relief resold or traded the meal they had received. In an effort to prevent this, Captain Darley, the Union inspector suggested that the meal be wet before being distributed so it would have to be consumed immediately.[90]

In May 1848, a public meeting was called to discuss the mismanagement of poor law union affairs. The conduct of the relieving officer for Ballymackey, William Young was discussed. It was claimed by Fr Power, a local priest that Young was not carrying out his duties. He claimed that Young had employed a local man, Pat Higgins to act as his deputy in Ballymackey and was paying him by giving him meal belonging to the union. Young denied this and said that Higgins was receiving meal because he had a sore foot. Young was supported by the guardian for the area, Richard Coughlan. However, Fr Power who obviously had knowledge of the local situation claimed that Higgins was a smith and also worked for Coughlan. At this point, Coughlan admitted this was true. Even though Young was obviously incompetent and the local guardian was covering for him, the other guardians at the meeting decided to acquit him of the charge of not fulfilling his duties.[91] This example of blatant corruption does not inspire any great confidence in the guardians management of poor relief.

Throughout 1848, Nenagh Union found it increasingly difficult to collect the rates which financed the workhouse and relief efforts. The poor rate for Aghnameadle had increased from 10d. in every pound in September 1846 to a peak of 5s. 6d. in May 1847. The poor rate for Ballymackey increased similarly from 7 ½d. in the pound in September 1846 to 4s. 6d. in May 1847. When new guardians for the Union were nominated that year, only three were found to be eligible as they were the only ones that had paid their rates in full. The paying of rates in Toomevara was further complicated when the rate collector for the electoral divisions of Aghnameadle and Ballymackey, Michael Carroll stole £100 of rates and fled to America.[92] Patrick Kennedy replaced him as the rate collector from September 1848 onwards.[93]

The situation worsened further when the potato crop throughout the area completely failed in 1848.[94] The numbers in the workhouse increased from 1,217 in January to 2,295 in October. Bridget Morrissey and Catherine Hennessey were indicted for stealing a small quantity of potatoes from James Willington.[95] Thomas Tracey recalled: 'To describe the pangs of hunger I witnessed among the people is out of my power, though I have now [1906] a distinct recollection so vividly was it impressed on my mind at the time'. He had seen the people 'feed in weeds, nettles, water grasses, and turnip tops'.[96] A local vet who is now one of the oldest living people from the parish of Toomevara can remember his grandfather talking about bringing loads of turnips on a horse and car to the village of Toomevara and turning them out on the street for the poor to eat during the Famine.[97] Amidst the suffering endured by some, life seems to have continued largely uninterrupted for others. The spring fair in 1848 was reported to be 'one of the best fairs that was held in Nenagh for a long time'.[98] The annual Lough Derg Regatta was held in September where the lake was 'studded with sailing craft of all descriptions'.[99] There was a small measure of help provided by some locals. Yellow meal was given to some poor people who weren't able to buy it at a house near Ollatrim mill in Toomevara.[1] However, it is unclear how long this continued or what year during the Famine it occurred.

The year 1849 brought even more misery for the lower classes of Toomevara with another year of potato blight.[2] In January, it was reported that 'in the electoral divisions of Toomevara, a second Skibbereen, there are about 1,000 persons, more than half the population in the most destitute circumstances'.

An old woman, named Catherine Marmion was found dead on the side of the road at Clonalea; she had died from exposure and starvation. In February, another woman, Winifred Mackey of Ballymackey also died from starvation and was found at the side of the road at Ballymackey. Throughout the wider district the situation was replicated. The *Nenagh Guardian* newspaper reported that in January and the beginning of February, five or six people had died of absolute starvation.[3] In May the *Nenagh Guardian* reported:

> Destitution is everyday becoming more appalling and widespread in this fertile but pauperised union. Groups of half starved looking creatures patrol the streets daily, begging for food and hundreds of men and women, who not many months ago were able bodied and well looking, might be seen covered with miserable rags, wending their way to the workhouse, either in slow straggling steps, or conveyed in donkey carts.[4]

It was reported that families in receipt of outdoor relief secretly buried their children who had died at night 'without coffins or shrouding, so, that they might thereby receive their rations'. In Nenagh union, the number receiving outdoor relief increased from 7,580 on 24 February, 1849 to 10,647 by April.[5]

The spread of cholera then became a further problem. From March 1849, it was on the increase in the Nenagh Union and the guardians decided to take a house separate to the fever hospital for the treatment of cholera patients.[6] Cholera sufferers from Toomevara would have to endure the journey of seven miles to Nenagh probably on foot to receive any treatment. Those who could, left the area, but as the newspaper report below suggests it was only those who could afford to do so.

> the tide of emigration flows rapidly from every town, village, hamlet and parish in this part of the county. The most industrious and comfortable farmers are disposing of their farms and converting their cattle, implements of husbandry and every particle of their property into money for the purpose of emigrating immediately to America and of quitting a land of pauperism and excessive taxation.[7]

Thomas Tracey noted that the cost was quite high and this 'debarred thousands from emigrating'.[8]

The number of evictions continued to increase throughout the Famine years with Tipperary having one of the highest rates of evictions throughout the whole country.[9] There were seven evictions recorded on the Cole Bowen estate in Ballymackey during 1848.[10] It was reported that 15 houses on the Massy Dawson estate were levelled by the sheriff and the occupants dispossessed that same year.[11] Those who took lands from which other tenants had been evicted often became victims of agrarian unrest. The repercussions varied from threatening notices, and assaults to property and animals being attacked. Jack Dwyer of Kilinafinch received a notice threatening him with death if he did not give up some land he had taken in June 1846. In July 1848 six men broke into the house of Thomas Meagher of Aghnameadle and a threatening notice was posted there warning him to give up the land upon which he was caretaker or he would be killed. John O'Brien of Aghnameadle had his skull cracked in three places after being beaten for taking a farm from which a family had been evicted in March 1849. Threatening notices were often displayed in public places such as the one posted on a tree in the chapel yard in Toomevara in May 1849 warning people not to graze the land of Monanore or any of Massy Dawson's property from which tenants had been evicted. Animals that belonged to the offender were often killed or maimed as a warning; at Clash in May 1848, the ears of five donkeys were cut off with the intention of intimidating the owners and preventing them taking some ground.[12]

Those who were responsible for evicting tenants were also the target of these types of crimes. In August 1848 a horse belonging to Edward Short of Pallas valued at £20 was shot in repercussion for his eviction of tenants. An attempt was made to kill land agent George Garvey of Thornvale as he had evicted numerous tenants in November 1847. An assassination attempt was also made on his under steward and bailiff, Denis Meara the following year. A house which Patrick Cummins of Toomevara had taken in July 1848 from which a family had been evicted was burned down.[13]

Despite the conditions of the time, the rent charged on the Cole Bowen estate in Ballymackey in 1849 increased.[14] There was a large amount of movement on the estate with holdings becoming available where tenants had either left or had been evicted. Of the 149 tenants recorded on the estate, nine were evicted, nine tenants' holdings were taken by new tenants, nine tenants' arrears were forgiven and five holdings were amalgamated with others. The arrears owed by the evictees ranged from zero to £178 7s. 0d. Those whose arrears were forgiven ranged from just over £2 to £22. It is interesting to note that some of those tenants whose arrears were forgiven owed more than some of the tenants who were evicted. This raises questions about what other factors were at play which determined the fate of families. Three of the tenants that were evicted owed no arrears.

By mid-1849, life for the poorer people in Toomevara was extremely bleak. They had suffered successive years of blight, starvation and fever. Employment opportunities were minimal and many were dependent on outdoor relief. Emigration as a means of escape was only an option for those who could afford it and those who could not were faced with a choice of the workhouse or starvation. In contrast, life for others such as land owners and larger farmers seems to have continued without the dramatic upheaval experienced by the poorer classes. For the latter, worse was to come.

3. Clearance

In May 1848, Richard Ievers Wilson replaced William Middleton of Toomevara as land agent on the Massy Dawson estate.[1] At the time, most of Toomevara village was in the hands of middlemen with very few of the tenants paying directly to the landlord, Massy Dawson.[2] It appears that when Wilson took over as land agent, he leased much of the village from Massy Dawson for a period of 20 years. Until this point, it seems that while the middlemen collected the rent from their tenants they did not in turn pay the rent they owed to Massy Dawson leading to high arrears on the village.[3] This came to a head on 24 May 1849 with the arrival of the 'crow bar brigade'.[4]

> The times were very bad and some men were willing to perform menial offices for money under the name of the 'Crow' or as they were called 'Crow bar brigade', well about 20 of these came out from Nenagh, escorted and guarded by police and military and in the early morning commenced their cruel work.[5]

Sixty constabulary from Nenagh under the command of Charles G. O'Dell left the town on Thursday morning. Samuel Murray Gason was sent by the sheriff's office and at 9.30 a.m. commenced taking over possession of the houses and cabins.[6] It seems that the evictions were to be carried out on Wednesday but for some reason they were postponed until Thursday.[7] John Donoghue, the under agent and bailiff, was also present. Between 40 and 50 cabins were levelled resulting in the eviction of over 500 people. Thomas Treacy, who witnessed the clearance, recalled it:

> It was a mournful sight, women carrying their younger children, fathers going frantic, the cries and roars could be heard a long distance perhaps four miles. I call now to mind the sight very clearly, long levers were used mostly crow bars, the under parts were undermined and the roof fell in with a crash.[8]

A reporter from the *Nenagh Vindicator* was present in Toomevara on the day of the evictions and described what he saw. The tenants of Henry Long who lived between Fr Meagher's house at the cross up as far as Mrs Hill's coach office which is now the pharmacy in Toomevara had 'thrown down their houses by arrangement in anticipation of the sheriff's arrival as they were promised the timber and thatch':

Leabharlanna Poiblí Chathair Bhaile Átha Cliath
Dublin City Public Libraries

It was a piteous spectacle on Thursday, in the midst of the pouring rain, to see children led by their parents out from their houses into the street, to see mothers kneel down on the wet ground and holding their children up to Heaven, beg relief from the Almighty and strength to endure their afflictions. The cries of bereaved women and men running half frantic through the streets or cowering from the rain and wind, under the shelter of their poor furniture piled confusedly about were affecting in the extreme. To see amid all this misery ten or twelve burly ruffians from Nenagh assailing the houses with crow-bars, and to hear their cries of exultation as a wall yielded to their assaults, or a roof tumbled down with a crash, the spectator should be callous that could avoid being greatly affected by the scene. It was altogether as deplorable a spectacle as I have ever beheld.[9]

At the upper end of Church Street, the sub sheriff's deputy Samuel Murray Gason, police, bailiffs and John Donoghue evicted 12 families from their houses. They levelled two of them and secured the doors on the others to prevent families returning.

After the work had been completed on the west end of the village near Fr Meagher's house and on Church Street, the bailiffs moved onto Main Street. They first took possession of some untenanted houses and then began to clear the tenants out of the other houses. On Main Street, 'some of the houses contained four and five families all in great destitution; they were scarcely half clad, and many of them had apparently got up from their miserable pallets of straw to go out on the road and lay their bodies in the ditch'. One man who was pushed out of a house by the bailiffs was 'a wretched looking creature … with gaunt and fleshless jaws, and eyes of most unnatural size and hideous wildness, greedily devouring some repulsive looking substance like paste from a metal pot which he held in his arms'.

While this man was being evicted, the sound of windows breaking in a house was heard further up Main Street where the bailiffs had not yet reached. A 'strong and comfortable looking man' was carrying furniture out of a house 'which was painted neatly, and presented an air of comfort in comparison with the other houses in the village'. His name was Andrew Gleeson and he was married with one child. Gleeson was complaining bitterly that he was going to be evicted even though he had a bake house and six acres and was doing well. At that, he was punched in the face by a local butcher. The reporter later heard that the butcher was due to get Gleeson's house after he was evicted. Gleeson stated he had paid £12 15s. within the previous three months for the house and he produced the receipts he had received from Donoghue, the driver and under agent on the estate.

The houses on Main Street from the corner up as far as a comfortable two storey house belonging to Brislanes were not levelled. However, when the

bailiffs started their work on Feather Street, past Brislanes, a group of bailiffs
came out from a house carrying a crow bar and commenced knocking the
houses there: 'Three or four of them would collect at a corner of a house and
by a few well directed strokes of the crow dislodge a quoin, when the wall
generally tumbled in an exceedingly brief short space of time'. They knocked
four houses and were applying crow bars to the wall of the fifth when it was
announced that a man named Booth was inside unable to leave his bed. Gason
entered and saw a 'poor creature on a wretched straw pallet in the corner, his
face and limbs were swollen, and he was scarcely able to articulate a word from
excessive debility'. Gason is said to have given him a shilling and appointed
him 'caretaker' of the house for a week. Thomas Treacy recalled two houses
that escaped levelling. A widow, Mary Connolly held these two houses. To her
advantage, she worked as a nurse to the Meagher family of Monanore. Michael
Meagher who was coroner for North Tipperary at the time used his influence
and sorted the matter out with Wilson and as a result, her houses were spared.[10]

Over 500 people were evicted in total on the day of the clearance: from
the Main Street, families included Brislanes, Britts, Devanny, Donoghues,
Doyles, Fitzpatricks, Gavins, Gilmartins, Gleesons, Hartys, Hares, Mahers,
O'Mearas, Powers, Quirkes, Rigneys, Shelleys, Shinners, Shorts, Tierneys and
Whelans; on Church Street Cahills, Crimmins, Cusacks, Fogartys, Hollands,
Malones, McDermotts, McGraths, O'Briens, Ryans and Whelans; and from
Feather Street Booths, Brislanes, Kellys and Larkins.

Thomas Treacy recalled that after the clearance was over, houses had been
cleared from the parochial house at the cross on the west side of the village
through to Church Street and along Main Street and Feather Street (both of
which are now known as Chapel Street).[11] 'The priest's house at the cross was
a splendid thatched cottage and out houses, the front door and windows facing
the Nenagh road, and occupied by the Revd Father Meagher P.P. who was
almost idolized by the parishioners many of whom were his own near friends.'[12]

AFTERMATH

When the clearances were over, the evicted were left with a few of their
belongings standing in the rain with nowhere to go. It had commenced raining
at about 12 o'clock and continued right through until evening:

> About 5 p.m. the work was over, the place in ruins and the only roof
> for souls was the vault of heaven. The people gathered their fragments
> of furniture, doors, dressers, old boxes and built sheds along the channel
> of chapel wall and school house, a few in the school house yard and the
> gardens at the rear of the two houses in Chapel street, which owing to
> some clause in writing escaped the tumbling.[13]

It was recorded as 'heartrending, absolutely terrific, to describe the contrivances resorted to in order to ward off the pelting of the pitiless storm':

> Chairs were arranged in squares, quilts, sheets, and pieces of old canvas were stretched on poles; wigwams were thus formed under whose covering the poor creatures were seated, completely saturated with the rain which fell through the flimsy awning overhead nearly as plentifully as it did from the skies without. Asses' cars, and turf baskets were also upturned, and gave shelter to scores of half clad wretches.[14]

There was not enough room for all the families to put up temporary shelters along the chapel walls or school house. Some families resorted to putting up a shelter over their family graves as they were not allowed on the village square. It was the property of the landlord. One family, the Devanys built a hut over their family grave and lived there until they moved to Moneygall later in the year.[15] These families who erected huts against the chapel walls were Bevans, Burns, Cartys, Devanys, Fords, Gavins, Hassetts, Keeshans, Kellys, Kennedys, Leonards, Lynches, Mahers, Purcells, Shinners, three Brislane families and two Ryan families.[16] Thomas Treacy remarked that each family had their own temporary hut; these were mainly made from some old boards and doors. This was all they had 'to keep out the inclemency of the weather' and all were obliged to stretch in straw in their clothes during the night. This was the only option available to the evictees. As Thomas Treacy recalled:

> The times then and now are as different as sin and virtue for then no one generally speaking could give you shelter when once the vengeance of landlord or agent was executed by eviction. Now and for years past if any one was evicted they find friendly shelter in a neighbour's house or a domicile erected close to this dwelling but then under threat of landlord or a gent there was nothing but the workhouses which were filled from floor to ceilings, and it was such a reproach to be called a 'poor house pauper' that the people suffered starvation and death sooner than enter.[17]

Thomas Treacy's recollections in 1906 are interesting from the point of view of how the social memory of the Famine impacted on his attitudes and also the perceived differences he saw in terms of development since the Land War and Plan of Campaign of the 1880s.

Most of the tenants in the village held under three middlemen who were also evicted. One of these middlemen was Denis McCarthy. He had been evicted six years previously when he had owed a large amount of money but was later allowed back on the estate. Other middlemen that were evicted were

Pat Hodgens and Henry Long who it was reported both owed five-and-a-half years rent. Pat Hodgens was reported to be the 'village lawyer – a class of persons generally held in estimation by the people, in proportion to their knowledge of legal quibbles, and other scheming propensities'.[18] A woman, Anne Hassett was evicted also. Like Denis McCarthy, she had been evicted previously. It was reported that she had owed £100 when first evicted but managed to get back on the estate and had leased 20 acres of land.[19] A reporter who went to see the devastation in the village after the clearance met her and some other evictees. She produced signed rent receipts she had received from Wilson, although it was noted that these receipts were on unstamped paper.[20] She also showed stamped rent receipts she had received from two former land agents on the estate, James O'Meara and Henry Chinnery. The *Nenagh Guardian* later tried to justify the clearing of tenants who had actually paid their rent by stating that 'it is well known that if there were one hundred tenants holding from a defaulting middleman on any one portion of a property or estate, they should, according to law, be evicted as well as he'.[21]

The *Nenagh Guardian* reported that 'we believe it is Mr Dawson's intention to repair the houses left standing, and also to improve the whole town, by building a better description of dwellings in it'.[22] However, there was no evidence to suggest this was true and no efforts were made to rebuild better housing. Thomas Treacy described Wilson as the villain in the process. No clearances took place on the rest of Massy Dawson's estate in South Tipperary.[23] Thomas Treacy said that 'the landlord Massy Dawson was not to blame as the town was in a measure let to the notorious Wilson, who exercized his severity on the inhabitants'. He described Wilson as 'one of the most notorious characters that ever lived who took a devilish delight in eviction, and scattering the honest, virtuous people of the village broadcast on the face of the earth'.[24]

When a reporter from the *Tipperary Vindicator* went to Toomevara after the clearance, he found many of those who had been evicted starving and trying to survive in terrible conditions.

> it is altogether impossible to do anything like justice to the dreadful scene that presented itself to our astonished gaze. Talk of Skibbereen, of Schull, of Ballinrobe, of all the black spots on the chequered map of our most ill fated country, on all the places which have obtained world wide notoriety for horror. Toomevara throws them completely in the shade – because in Toomevara there are none of the appearances, so far of the decorum of civilization – society seems to have been shattered to pieces – huts of the most wretched possible description were made up against the chapel walls – low, without ventilation, room, or any one convenience fit for human habitations some of them not five feet square.[25]

Ignatius O'Leary, the relieving officer provided whatever provisions the Board of Guardians would permit. When the reporter reached Feather Street, he saw the remains of the knocked huts and was told that the former inhabitants were now 'in the ditches in the adjacent townlands, wherever a dry nook or an overhanging tree afforded a favourable situation for re-erecting a hut'.

REACTION

Media reaction to the clearance was varied. *The Times* called it 'one of the most sweeping clearances of tenantry that has yet been recorded in the annals of southern evictions'.[26] The *Evening Post* reported that they never 'heard of so sweeping and so crushing an expulsion as this, in a single day, upon a portion of the property of one proprietor'.[27] The *Nenagh Guardian*'s political bias was evident in its reports. As mentioned earlier it was a conservative Protestant publication. Its first report on the clearances on 26 May 1849 was particularly scathing of the inhabitants of Toomevara and expressed the opinion that the clearances were really the proper course of action.[28] It reported that the people living in Toomevara were 'vile characters', the place had 'got into a most disorganized condition' and Mr Dawson had not received any rent. It claimed that when Dawson's agent applied for the rent, he received a threatening letter through the post. It also reported that Wilson had used 'every conciliatory means in his power with the tenants'. The comment which later caused much outrage was that 'The greater portion of the village has been a plague-spot on the estate – it was the resort of all evicted tenants from neighbouring estates – in short, it was in part a den of midnight thieves and highway robbers'. This was backed up with the claim that at that time there were 'six or seven men from that town in Nenagh gaol for cow-stealing' and even that the parish priest's pig and his boots had recently been stolen. However, the report laid most of the blame on the middlemen for not paying the rent.

Following a highly critical report in the *Tipperary Vindicato*r and the national outcry which followed the clearances, the *Nenagh Guardian* softened their opinion and wrote that they 'did not of course include the entire village in the same category with those who lived by plunder.' They emphasized that the most blame for the clearances lay with the middlemen and their actions 'left no other course to be adopted but that which the Revd Massy Dawson was obliged to pursue'. They stated that Dawson was only 'asserting his rights' and, indeed, the clearances were advantageous to all as:

> large tracts of land which had been dotted over with miserable mud
> cabins, occupied by the poorest classes, who lived by begging, and the
> pittance of out door relief they received, may now be seen cultivated

and properly tilled, instead of being waste and useless – and the occupiers have become residents of the poor house, where they have comfortable and regular diet. It was a charity to those people to compel them to enter the Union Poor House, for if they had a strip of land they could neither till it, nor pay for it – it was an encumbrance to them, and but increased their wretchedness and poverty, as well as being the primary cause of engendering disease and plague.[29]

In contrast, the *Tipperary Vindicator* expressed dismay and shock at the events and asked: 'Is the law to permit a whole village to be swept away after this fashion, the occupants of it to be unhoused and misery unparalleled to over spread the country in a time of sickness and peril?'[30]

RELIEF EFFORTS

Relief efforts to help those who were evicted appear to have been limited. The parish priest, Fr Meagher appeared to be the only person who responded quickly. In the immediate aftermath of the clearance, he left the village for Dublin where he secured £20 from the Dublin General Relief Committee. It was reported on 6 June that Wilson had asked Fr Meagher to advise the evicted to leave the village and go to the workhouse.[31]

After receiving a letter from Fr Meagher, the Poor Law Commissioners sent a letter to the Nenagh Board of Guardians about providing workhouse accommodation in or near Toomevara for those who were evicted.[32] A full two weeks after the clearances on 9 June, Captain Drought the inspector of the Union went to Toomevara and took a house at Grawn, near Toomevara to provide shelter for those who were evicted. This house was reported to be 'one of the most commodious in or near the village' where the Widow Kennedy had resided.[33] However, the relieving officer said that the able bodied would not go into the workhouse or this house in Toomevara. It was reported in the *Tipperary Vindicator* that a great many of the able bodied 'spread and scattered throughout the country'. Matt Hayes, another guardian said that 'poor, miserable and clothed in rags as they are, they carry about them natural modesty and female delicacy. They would not like to be congregated together in this house'. However, out of utter desperation, 120 people later sheltered there 'in the direst confusion and most disgusting disorder'.[34] At least 40 of the able-bodied evictees applied for outdoor relief but this was refused. Thomas Treacy remarked that as it was harvest time soon after the evictions 'the inhabitants of the huts were able to provide just the very necessaries to keep body and soul together' and they 'clung to the very huts, as an elysium'.[35]

LIFE AFTER THE CLEARANCE

They also seem to have organized themselves to warn others against taking up the evicted properties and holdings; for example a number of cows which were grazing on land owned by Massy Dawson at Monanore were attacked; on the 14 June, a large cock of straw, two door frames and other articles belonging to Michael Grace of Toomevara were set on fire and burned. Grace had taken land from Massy Dawson from which a man named Kelly had been evicted.[36] Despite the fact that the village had been almost destroyed and hundreds of people were left homeless, life continued as normal for many farmers in the local area. The fair in Toomevara went ahead only four days after the clearance. While farmers at this time were not thriving, there were some around Toomevara who were obviously coping well enough to have stock to sell. It was reported that the following month another fair took place in Toomevara at which there was 'a good show of stock of every description which went off at ruinously low prices'.[37]

There was further worry ahead for the residents of Toomevara during the autumn when news spread that the potato crop had once again failed. The *Nenagh Guardian* described the survival of the potato crop that year as 'the last or only hope of the labouring poor of Ireland'. To make matters worse for the poorest, it was decided within the Union to cease outdoor relief in August 1849.[38] This spelled disaster for those who had been dependent on outdoor relief. Nationally, the harvest of 1849 was mostly healthy with isolated instances of blight.[39] However Tipperary along with Clare and Kerry were the most severely hit.[40]

'HUT TUMBLERS'

By February 1850, many of the evicted remained on in their makeshift huts. Thomas Treacy recalled how those who had settled in the huts tried to get on with everyday life.

> In the long evenings there were the neighbours, [who] collected and passed away their time to some innocent amusement, such as dancing, singing, story telling etc. They subsisted on the humblest fare, Indian meal stirabout with water in which sugar was dissolved, sometimes sugar over the stirabout and eaten relish – poor religious, light hearted souls.[41]

Treacy remembered how Bianconi coaches passing through Toomevara on the Dublin to Limerick route had a team of horses stabled in Toomevara at the back of what is now the local pharmacy and two adjoining houses. While the horses were being changed, it was common for the passengers to alight to look at the huts and people and in many cases distribute relief.[42]

On the morning of 20 February 1850, John Donoghue called on a number of local men who were tenants on the Massy Dawson estate to come to his house in the village.[43] Thomas Treacy recalled that those involved included numerous Donoghues, three O'Meara families, Keatys, Kennedys, Delaneys and two men by the surnames of Leo and Brown.[44] It appears that many of them partook of drinks when they arrived at his house.[45] James O'Meara, one of the group of tenants at Donoghue's house and a former land agent on the estate himself was sent by Donoghue to tell the hut owners to give up possession of their huts peaceably.[46] At around two o'clock Donoghue led the group of men to the huts. Thomas Treacy recalled that 'the town was deserted. There were some four men, some women and a lot of boys, girls and children' present.[47] It was claimed that Donoghue called on his men to stand, raise up stones and follow him and tumble the huts in spite of any man in Tipperary. The group of men led by Donoghue proceeded to level the makeshift huts whereupon a struggle took place. One of the hut's inhabitants, Johnny Gavin and John Donoghue engaged in a struggle and a scythe owned by Gavin was used during the struggle. The local police were called upon and it was later reported that 'only that the police were called out and the peace preserved, the consequences would be frightful'. The matter was brought before the Nenagh petty sessions and a case of grievous assault was brought against John Gavin by John Donoghue, Johnny Donoghue, Mike Donoghue, Bill O'Meara, James O'Meara, Matt O'Meara, Michael Delaney, John Delaney and Ned Brown. From the evidence given in court, some more details of the days events become clear.

John Donoghue claimed that he had taken it upon himself to tumble the huts but he had done so on the authority of Massy Dawson and according to the desire of the parish priest Fr Meagher. He claimed he was being deprived of tolls on fair days in Toomevara due to the location of some of the makeshift huts and for this reason he decided to tumble them. He swore that he had 30 men with him whom he had treated to a glass of whiskey at his house before hand. John Gavin swore that the men had the appearance of being intoxicated, a claim which was repeated by the head constable in Toomevara, King. He said

> They appeared excited and were almost in a drunken state. They appeared as if they were after drinking. I consider it was not proper of Donoghue to bring men in an excited and drunken state to tumble those huts.[48]

Donoghue claimed that when tumbling the huts, John Gavin followed him and struck him on the side of the head with a scythe. He could think of no reason why Gavin would do such a thing 'unless for being a bailiff to the estate of Mr Dawson'. However, John Gavin claimed that Donoghue had assaulted him before he struck him. He claimed to have had a scythe in his hands at this time which he was about to put inside the chapel wall for safety when he was struck by Donoghue. He claimed that James O'Meara then hit him with a stone after which Donoghue knocked him against the side of a hut and got seven or eight of his men to hit him. It appears that at some time during the altercation the scythe struck Donoghue. Johnny Gavin's wife Sally and a neighbour, Biddy Lynch, both claimed they had seen Donoghue strike Gavin first. Sally Gavin claimed that she had called out to them not to kill the father of her children and that some of Donoghue's party who were drunk attacked her and she ran to Head Constable King for protection. James O'Meara testified on Donoghue's behalf and said that he himself had no stone in his hand when going to level the huts but after Donoghue was struck the group 'stooped for stones'. He said he saw Donoghue engage with Gavin but he 'certainly saw Gavin strike him first'.[49] King stated that Donoghue as bailiff and driver was 'a very decent man' and Gavin was a 'hard working young man'. A case against Gavin for grievous assault was returned to the Thurles Quarter Sessions. The Bench admonished Donoghue for giving whiskey to his party and said it was 'highly improper' of him. Gavin was bound to keep the peace as Donoghue claimed that 'on my oath I am afraid of being shot in the street by Gavin and the other evicted tenants'. For generations, the families involved including those of Donoghue were known locally as 'hut tumblers'.[50]

As Donoghue's party was made up of tenants on the estate, their best interests would have been served by keeping in Donoghue and Wilson's favour. Thomas Treacy recorded that there were always people at the time who wanted to gain favour with those in a position of power.[51] Whether they came to Donoghue's house that morning voluntarily or under duress is unclear. Their possible motivation was to avoid the same fate themselves. Thomas Treacy recalled that his own father had been offered a place in Toomevara if he would help tumble the huts. However, he refused and as a result they were forced to leave Toomevara. They got a house in nearby Moneygall and the family moved there. Even if many of the party were under duress to take part in the hut tumbling, it is clear that most of the party enjoyed a few drinks that morning at Donoghue's house. This begs the question; was the drink a ploy on Donoghue's behalf to persuade them to do his bidding, or were they all willing participants whose self-interest overrode their concern for more unfortunate neighbours?

After the huts were tumbled, the evicted families were left to face the same plight as they had eight months before. Thomas Treacy recalled that at least 20 families had lived in these huts; however it is unclear how many were tumbled by Donoghue.[52] Many families went to settle in neighbouring towns.[53] It is believed locally that many of these families moved to Moneygall and found accommodation there. John Leo was given a house for his part in the hut tumbling and was also later given a job as caretaker on the Massy Dawson estate.[54] In May 1850, when he called to William O'Meara's house near Toomevara, a group of men broke into the house, assaulted him, smashed the windows and fled.[55] A shot was fired into James O'Meara's house on 2 September 1851 for taking a house from which a tenant had been evicted. A notice was also posted on the door threatening him and his brother with assassination unless they gave up the house.[56] As outlined earlier, taking a house or land where someone had been evicted usually caused a lot of trouble for the new tenant. In many cases, it was outsiders who were brought in to take up such holdings. However, James O'Meara who appears to have been a friend of Donoghues and stood as a witness for him at the petty sessions trial obviously felt secure enough to risk such action.

John Donoghue was called to the Insolvent Debtors court in Nenagh on 6 December 1850 by a miller, James McDonnell, and John Egan. He owed McDonnell £20 for flour and meal which he had refused to pay. At this time Donoghue was described as the post master, pound keeper, under agent for Revd Massy Dawson, shop keeper and hotel keeper. There was much laughter in the court when Toomevara was referred to as an extensive and flourishing town. The witness, James Stapleton said that Toomevara was flourishing until the tumbling of the houses. The court declared that Donoghue was a 'very improper person after this exposé, to be pound-keeper and those who appoint him as such do so at their own risk'.[57]

Of the 'hut tumblers', Thomas Treacy remarked that there were only a few of their families remaining in the parish by 1906.[58] It has been ascertained that the descendants of four of these men still live or own land in the parish to this day.[59] James O'Meara who was a land agent prior to the clearances came to own numerous properties in the village of Toomevara and some land. Matt O'Meara and his family were forced to leave their farm and move to a smaller farm of poorer quality nearby. James O'Meara, the former land agent was given the farm that Matt O'Meara had originally occupied. The descendants of the third man, Bill O'Meara still own land in the parish to this day. There are also some descendents of the Donoghues living in the parish. A direct descendant of the Donoghues recently returned to Ireland to trace his ancestors and aghast at learning what had occurred, sent a letter to the local paper detailing the experience and said: 'What was uncovered did shock me; you cannot chose your ancestors'.[60] One of John Donoghue's sons, also called John, emigrated to Australia in 1853 at the age of 22. He was never known to contact his Irish family or speak of them and this in particular led his descendant to research the family's origins.

Stories which have survived tell of some of the more innocent ways in which the villagers sought revenge on Wilson. Wilson had a short leg and an iron foot to enable him to walk. A local man, Tommy Ryan (Nailer) as he was known, had a pup with a short leg and called him Wilson. Wilson himself frequently travelled on the stage coach and apparently, Tommy used to walk down to the coach office and call out 'Wilson little dog, you cripple, come on, the horses are yoked' and other comments. Apparently, Wilson used to laugh it off but later made unsuccessful efforts to clear Tommy from the village. Thomas Treacy recorded a number of planned attempts which were made on Wilson's life but these were never carried to fruition. The hatred and bitterness felt towards Wilson can be seen in the stories that surrounded his death. When he died, his flesh was said to have 'melted away' and he 'was a mass of corrupt matter so that he could scarcely be coffined'.[61]

4. After the clearance

The clearance in the village of Toomevara was not an isolated occurrence. While there were undoubtedly many individual evictions throughout the parish, it was only the larger-scale ones which were reported. In the period between the main clearance in May 1849 and the 'hut tumbling', a number of other incidents occurred. A couple of days after the clearances in the village of Toomevara, Gason, the sub sheriff's deputy carried out another eviction and levelling in nearby Kilinafinch. Five families consisting of 33 people, mostly children, were evicted from their properties which were owned by James Willington of Castle Willington, Ballymackey. The families involved were Quigleys, Magans and three Quirke families. A widow and her large family were also to be evicted but the widow, Mrs Ryan was very ill. The bailiffs 'caught the sheets of the bed by the corners and in this mode carried her into the open air'. Mrs Ryan was 'a miserable spectacle of the ravages of a wasting sickness and had so wretched an appearance that Gason, the executioner of the law, directed her to be brought back to her bed and allowed to remain under the shelter of her own roof'.[1] The Ryans were not subsequently evicted and their descendants live in the parish today.[2] In late August 1849, five people were evicted at Latteragh from land which was the property of the earl of Orkney.[3]

There were incidences in the parish where the victims tried to resist or regain what they had lost. However, these were mainly people who either had the means to do so or had the back up of other neighbours or friends. One such example occurred in early September. Fifty men accompanied a man named Kennedy to a farm in Ballymackey from which his father had been evicted. The farm was the property of Henry Cole Bowen of Bowenscourt, Co. Cork. They cut down an acre-and-a-half of wheat and, even though the police were called and a fight ensued, the men managed to get away with some of the wheat. In October of that year, another incident occurred. A bailiff in Toomevara, Cummins seized two cows, horses, 17 geese and a winnowing machine from a farmer for non payment of rent and put them in the pound in Toomevara. He was about to sell these when a large crowd assembled at the pound. The land agent, John Donoghue, who was also the pound keeper opened the gate and allowed the stock to be carried away. While it is unclear who owned the objects seized, it is certain that the owner was in league with

Donoghue. In October 1849, 17 cattle were seized from John Hunt's land for non payment of rent. The cattle in question actually belonged to his cousin Denis Crowe but had been grazing on Hunt's land. On 30 October at six o'clock in the morning, Denis Crowe, Phillip Russell and Thomas Ryan went to the pound at Kilinafinch and broke it open to release the cattle. When driving away the cattle, they met Patrick Kennedy who was a brother of the pound owner and they reportedly assaulted him and robbed him of a small pistol. This was reported to police in Latteragh. The Kennedys, a constable and four sub constables went in pursuit of the men and cattle. When they reached Cloncannon they found the cattle but could not see any person. However, when Michael Kennedy began to round up the cattle the group were attacked with stones fired by people hiding behind ditches and local houses. The police fired, but, as they were well outnumbered, they left the scene. The cattle were not recovered by the pound keeper.[4]

LAST YEARS OF THE FAMINE: 1850 AND 1851

The year 1851 is often regarded as marking the end of the Famine and while things were gradually improving, there were still signs of hardship and destitution in the area. In March 1850 there were 3,684 inmates in the workhouse and this high occupancy continued into the following year with 3,534 inmates recorded in March 1851.[5] There were many signs of hardship outside the workhouse. In February 1850 a woman from Kilkeary, Mary Corban, died on the roadside from starvation and exposure to the weather. Reports of this kind continued into the following year. In April 1851, James Coffey died on the roadside on Spout Road in Nenagh from 'extreme destitution and want'. In May 1851, a 70-year-old woman died from destitution in Nenagh. Later that month, a man named McCormack was admitted to the workhouse but was found dead the following morning from destitution. A woman named Peggy Ryan was found dead on the roadside near Dolla from destitution. In contrast to this, a fair in Nenagh in spring 1850 was 'well stocked and well attended by buyers, when considerable sales were effected'. It was reported in early summer that new potatoes were being sold in Nenagh market at 1½d. per pound. They were reportedly 'clean, of good size, healthy and substantial'. There were symptoms of blight in a few districts locally in 1850 and 1851 but for the most part the crops were fine.[6]

High emigration still continued and throughout 1850 numerous advertisements appeared in local newspapers offering opportunities for emigration to Australia and Buenos Aires. It was reported in April 1851 that the 'tide of emigration' was increasing daily in the district.[7] Nenagh workhouse sent three groups of young girls to Australia between 1849 and 1852. It was hoped that they would find employment and settle there while also ridding the poor law union of the burden of their keep. Not all of these girls were orphans, many had one parent who was unable to support them. Of the first group of 40 girls, five were from Toomevara.[8]

The Revd Massy Dawson died in 1851 and his brother Captain Dawson became the new owner of the estate. When he came to Toomevara in June 1851, 'tar barrels were lighted, and he was surrounded by all his tenants, who cheered him loudly and exhibited towards him other tokens of respect and esteem as a kind and good landlord'.[9] This was fairly standard reportage regarding such events. Without estate accounts it is difficult to ascertain how patriarchal he was but it was also reported that he 'gave abatements in the rents of some, and others particularly in Toomevara, he sent to America'. If this report is an accurate account of what happened, it shows that, as Thomas Treacy recorded, people did not hold the Dawsons responsible for the evictions and clearances in the village. A similar account of Count D'Alton's homecoming to Grennanstown in July 1851 was reported where 'the assemblage were regaled with substantial food and good drink'.[10]

CONSEQUENCES OF THE FAMINE

Population

While the Famine itself was coming to a close, it cannot be said that life resumed as normal. Life and landscape throughout the country had been irreversibly changed and the events of the previous six years had huge consequences for Toomevara as it had nationally. The Famine triggered a

Table 4.1. Population change in Toomevara, 1841–51[13]

Population Change, 1841–51

Area	Size (nearest acre)	1841 (Population)	1851 (Population)	Percentage decrease in population
Kilkeary	2,726	794	354	55.40
Latteragh	954	289	161	44.30
Aghnameadle	10,322	3,893	2,194	43.60
Ballymackey	9,713	3,178	1,947	38.70
Templedowney	1,839	552	346	37.30
Toomevara Parish	28,665	8,706	4,992	42.60
Upper Ormond	79,471	26,530	18,632	29.80
Tipperary	1,961,722	435,553	323,829	25.70

population decline that lasted well into the 20th century.[11] By mid-1851 about one million had died and another million had emigrated.[12] In this chapter when discussing population change between 1841 and 1851, the figures used are for the Roman Catholic parish of Toomevara and do not include data from the townlands in Latteragh which are not part of Toomevara parish.

In the 10-year-period between 1841 and 1851, the population of the parish declined by over 42%. When compared to the 29.8% population decline throughout the barony and 25.7% population decline throughout the county, it appears that Toomevara fared particularly badly. It should be noted Tipperary fared particularly badly during the Famine, experiencing the fourth-highest death rate throughout Ireland, after western counties Sligo, Galway and Mayo.[14]

Kilkeary suffered the highest percentage population decline at 55% while the civil parish of Aghnameadle numerically lost the most people. Aghnameadle is the largest civil parish in Toomevara with over 10,000 acres and also contains Toomevara village so this large population decrease was unsurprising. Toomevara village itself had a crippling population decrease of almost 53%, declining from 885 in 1841 to 419 in 1851.[15] The population decline in Aghnameadle excluding Toomevara village was 41%, which indicates that the decrease in the civil parish's total population is not solely as a consequence of the clearances in the village. Overall, each civil parish in Toomevara had a greater percentage population loss than both Upper Ormond and Tipperary.

While all civil parishes lost a large percentage of their population, examining individual townlands shows that the situation varied from townland to townland. Of the 95 townlands that comprise the parish of Toomevara, 76 (80%) of them had a population decrease, one (1%) remained the same and 18 (19%) had an increase in population between 1841 and 1851.[16]

Table 4.2. Townlands in Toomevara with largest percentage population decrease between 1841 and 1851[17]

Civil parish	Townland	Area (to the nearest acre)	Valuation 1851 (to nearest pound)	Total pop. 1841	Total pop. 1851	Percentage population decrease
Aghnameadle	Castlequarter	126	120	47	0	100.0
Aghnameadle	Baynanagh	131	70	167	8	95.2
Kilkeary	Ballinamona	439	194	93	10	89.2
Ballymackey	Clashnevin	380	145	211	24	88.6
Ballymackey	Garranthurles	51	23	47.0	10.0	78.7
Aghnameadle	Monanore	426	144	102.0	23.0	77.5
Aghnameadle	Glenawinna	126	46	31.0	8.0	74.2
Ballymackey	Garrynafana	363	163	191.0	52.0	72.8
Kilkeary	Knockbrack	169	70	172.0	48.0	72.1

Table 4.2 shows the 10 townlands with the largest population decline between 1841 and 1851. The population of these townlands decreased between 70% and 100%. While Toomevara village is recorded separately on the census reports, many houses which were cleared were located in townlands on the edge of the village such as Castlequarter, Baynanagh and Bunacum and this contributed to the severe population decrease in these townlands. Castlequarter had 47 inhabitants in 1841 but by 1851 was uninhabited. The other townlands that had high percentage population loss are scattered throughout the parish and do not show any particular trends in terms of size or valuation. However, almost all of these have relatively good quality land and are not located in any of the higher mountainous areas of the parish which is unusual, as poorer quality land was often associated with higher population loss.

Of the 18 townlands which had an increase in population between 1841 and 1851 in Toomevara, 50% were in Ballymackey, 22% in Aghnameadle 11% in Kilkeary and Latteragh and 6% in Templedowney. Table 4.3 shows the 10 with the highest increase in population in the parish. Ballymackey features strongly.

Table 4.3. Townlands in Toomevara with highest increase in population between 1841 and 1851[18]

Civil Parish	Townland	Area (to nearest acre)	Valuation 1851 (to nearest pound)	Total pop. 1841	Total pop. 1851	Increase in number of people
Ballymackey	Killowney, Little	559	350	60	94	(+34)
Ballymackey	Lismore	225	150	92	115	(+23)
Ballymackey	Gortnadrumman	164	61	18	36	(+18)
Ballymackey	Cloonmore	204	113	44	59	(+15)
Ballymackey	Kilgorteen	201	81	26	41	(+15)
Kilkeary	Ballcrenode	354	210	13	27	(+14)
Templedowney	Carrickmaunsell	136	77	41	54	(+13)
Ballymackey	Derrybane	113	56	12	24	(+12)
Aghnameadle	Killavalla	89	27	0	11	(+11)
Ballymackey	Killeisk	119	72	15	26	(+11)

Individual townlands with a population increase does not necessarily mean that they escaped the ravages of the Famine. The population increase in some of these townlands could well be explained by local family movement, household amalgamation or an increased number of births in a small number of families. Table 4.3 highlights that most of these townlands were located in

Ballymackey. As mentioned in chapter one, Ballymackey contained the best quality farming land in the parish and was where most of the gentry and large landowners resided. As the better off in general escaped the worst ravages of the Famine, the fact that the majority of the gentry in the parish lived in Ballymackey probably had an influence on certain townlands' population increase. For example, Killowney Little, the townland which had the highest population increase, was home to both John Willington and Captain Jackson. Both owned extensive land and houses in the parish.[19]

Direct deaths during the Famine as a result of starvation and infectious diseases have been well publicized. Indirect deaths 'due to the disruption of the normal operation of society' are often not considered.[20] An example of this is the births which would have occurred if the Famine had not occurred. Table 4.4 shows the number of Catholic baptisms in Toomevara between the years 1845 and 1856. The significant difference between the number of baptisms prior to the Famine and those during and after, highlight the number of births which would have probably come about if the Famine had not intervened. There were a total of 4,321 baptisms between the years 1832 and 1845 with an average of 309 each year.[21] In the following 10 years, there were 1,685 baptisms with an average of 153 each year. Surprisingly, there were a couple of years during the Famine where the number being baptized increased on the previous year such as 1848 and 1850. However, after 1850 the numbers plummeted and continued in a similar pattern showing the true impact of the Famine in relation to births in the parish.

Table 4.4. Number of Catholic baptisms in Toomevara parish, 1845–55[22]

Year	1845	1846	1847	1848	1849	1850	1851	1852	1853	1854	1855	1856
Catholic baptisms	350	274	263	287	150	213	94	87	74	95	81	67

On examining the parish records for the years prior to the Famine, a wide variety of surnames are listed. However, after the Famine it is evident that many of these surnames have disappeared. There are 187 surnames recorded in the parish baptism records between 1831 and 1852 which are not mentioned in the records again for the 19th century showing that these families either emigrated, moved to another area or did not survive the Famine. Some of these included Mannions, Meaneys, Meehans, Semples, Shortens, Straffords, Longs, Ormonds, Sextons, Tobins, Langtons, Doolins etc. Few of these surnames have reappeared in the 20th century but these are new families to the area.

Housing

On a national scale, housing across the country changed dramatically as a result of the Famine. Nationally, there was a decrease of almost 72% in fourth-class housing between 1841 and 1851 which amounted to 355,689 mud cabins disappearing from the landscape. This trend was mirrored in Tipperary with a 64% decrease in fourth-class housing, from 22,819 in 1841 to 8,201 in 1851.[23]

In the parish of Toomevara, the number of inhabited houses declined from 1,419 in 1841 to 824 in 1851, a decrease of 595 or 42%. Regarding the civil parishes, the changes in terms of housing were similar to the population changes. Table 4.5 shows the decrease in inhabited houses in each civil parish and shows that similar to the population loss in each civil parish, Aghnameadle had the largest decrease in absolute values while Kilkeary had the largest percentage decrease.

Table 4.5. Change in housing in Toomevara by civil parish, 1841–51[24]

	Inhabited houses 1841	Inhabited houses 1851	Decrease in housing
Kilkeary	123	51	72 (59%)
Latteragh	40	22	18 (45%)
Aghnameadle	612	348	264 (43%)
Ballymackey	545	335	210 (39%)
Templedowney	97	62	35 (36%)
Toomevara Parish	1417	818	599 (42%)

Again, at townland level the situation varied from one to another. Sixty-eight (71.6%) of townlands in Toomevara had a decrease in the number of inhabited houses, 14 (14.7%) had no change and 13 (13.7%) of townlands had an increase in the number of inhabited houses. The number of uninhabited houses in the same period increased by 34, from 16 to 50 which meant that allowing for the increase in uninhabited houses, 561 houses disappeared from the landscape in Toomevara between 1841 and 1851. The fact that so many houses completely disappeared in a 10-year-period indicates that they were either purposely cleared or were of such an unsubstantial character they disintegrated once they became unoccupied. This proves the well-highlighted point that it was the poorest in society – the landless labourer and cottiers – who were the most affected by the Famine and who were practically wiped out.

The General Valuation of 1850 provided valuations for each holding in the country and the details provided for Toomevara can be used to examine the types of houses that had survived the Famine. The average valuation of a house in the parish at this time was £1 14s.[25] A house of this value was far superior

to the typical fourth-class mud hut which characterized over 55% of houses
in Toomevara in 1841.[26] Table 4.6 shows the number and valuation of houses
in the parish in 1850. Thirty-one per cent of the housing was valued at less
than 10s. and was obviously of very poor quality and standard. While those
houses valued at under £1 in 1850 are not exactly comparable with fourth-
class housing in 1841, they would have included those houses which were
fourth class and possibly some of the third-class housing.

Table 4.6. Building valuation in Toomevara 1850[27]

Value of buildings	1s.– 10s.	11s.– £1	£1 1s.– £2	£2 1s.– £5	£5 1s.– £10	£10 1s. +
Number of holdings	262 (31%)	224 (27%)	166 (20%)	139 (16%)	33 (4%)	20 (2%)

The fate of those who had lived in the poorest type of housing in 1841
was limited to one of three options. It has been said that they died, migrated
to larger urban areas or possibly emigrated.[28] However as discussed earlier,
emigration was not a realistic option for those from the poorest echelons of
society or the poorest housing. This was generally limited to those from a
background with the means to emigrate. In Toomevara, the fate of the majority
of those who had lived in the houses which disappeared was undoubtedly
limited to death or migration to another area. While it may rest easier to
imagine that their inhabitants had migrated, 'the reality is more likely to be
found in the Famine graveyards'.[29] Those that survived were often in a better
position than they had been before the Famine as they were part of a smaller
population which did not face the same pressure and competition for access
to land and housing.[30]

   In the parish in 1850, the average value of houses which had land attached,
of which there were 503, was £2 10s.[31] In comparison, there were 343 houses
with no land or substantial gardens attached and the average value for these
buildings was 16s. The small standard deviation of both ranges suggests that
the averages are reliable. The substantial difference between the average value
of buildings on land holdings and those which did not include land indicates
that those people in the parish in 1850 who were land holders were living in
houses of superior standard and value to those non land holders.

Land valuation and holdings
The general valuation of 1850 shows that of the 727 land holdings in the parish
of Toomevara, they ranged in size from quarter acre gardens to a farm which
contained over 459 acres.[32] The average size of a holding in the parish was just

over 35 acres. This represented a substantial increase from the average landholding of 15 to 20 acres prior to the Famine. The standard deviation for the sample is quite large possibly indicating that this average may be slightly skewed by a small number of outlying values. However the sample's mode is between 20.1 and 50 acres. It has already been shown that those landholders in Toomevara who survived the Famine had higher quality housing. It appears that they also had larger farm sizes.

Evictions

At the peak of the Famine in 1849, 9,802 people were evicted from North Tipperary alone, 40% more than South Tipperary for the same period.[33] Tipperary in general experienced higher eviction rates than most other counties, having the fourth-highest eviction rate in the province for that year.[34] Examining the eviction rates over a longer period, it can be seen that Tipperary had one of the highest rates of evictions throughout the whole country both during and after the Famine.[35] The devastation that evictions and clearances created in Toomevara has been outlined earlier. Comparing a map of pre-Famine Toomevara with a map drawn in 1901 shows how certain parts of the village never recovered from the clearance with no evidence remaining of many of the houses which once stood (Appendix B).[36] Apart from the immediate effects suffered by those evicted, the village's population and landscape was irreversibly damaged. The high level of clearances in Tipperary played a part in higher emigration from the county.

Emigration

As stated earlier, it was generally felt that those who emigrated from north-west Tipperary during and after the Famine were not from the poorest level of society but from what was described as 'the better class'.[37] An exception to this was the government scheme of sending female orphans to Australia. Even though the population had decreased dramatically by 1851, emigration continued at a very high rate. Almost 18% of Tipperary's 1851 population emigrated in the following four years. This was the highest proportion of emigrants to leave any county in these years.[38] It was also likely that more people were encouraged to leave as positive reports arrived home from those who had already emigrated.[39] Testament to the numbers that actually emigrated from Toomevara is the steady stream of Americans and Australians who each year come to the parish or write to the local newspaper trying to trace their ancestors who left during or in the immediate aftermath of the Famine.

Social Memory

According to Woodham Smith 'the Famine left hatred behind. Between Ireland and England the memory of what was done and endured has lain like a sword'.[40] It is claimed that 'it is beyond questioning that the notions connecting huge food exports with mass starvation and British genocide became deeply rooted in folk memory'.[41] Donnelly maintains that it is the clearances, such as that in Toomevara which contributed more than any other events associated with the Famine 'to the generation and spread of anti–British hostility in Ireland and especially the Irish diaspora'.[42]

As well as hatred towards the English administration and landlords for their lack of assistance after 1847, there was a lot of bitterness felt towards those Irish who could have given more help during the Famine and towards those who took advantage of the dire predicament others found themselves in and used this for their own advancement. This is certainly suggested in the local lore and social memory of the Famine in Toomevara. As stated earlier in this chapter, the average size of a holding was much higher after the Famine than before. Many were able to secure larger holdings by taking land from the less fortunate who had been evicted or had left. In the 1930s this was still remembered with bitterness.

> During and after the Famine the greater part of the land especially the big farms changed hands. The owners were evicted and no locals would be got to take their lands. These then fell into the possession of imported bailiffs and grabbers, brought from distant parts. And it is their descendants who now possess the big farms of our parish. But the origin of these people is not forgotten. They lack the respect which goes to the poor descendants still living in hovels, of these people who kept their name and their honour and their loyalty to their neighbours, in those evil days of Famine and evictions.[43]

Comments such as: certain families were 'brought in' or 'came in on land' are used to describe some families' origins in the area. As has been documented, local families who took land from which others were evicted were often victims of threatening notices and attacks. However, according to local lore, other tactics were also adopted by locals such as certain families' stock being boycotted at fairs and markets.

These tactics obviously did not bother some in the parish. Proximity and friendship with those who were in positions of power and influence seem to have provided enough protection and security to render the threat of boycott or attacks meaningless. According to local lore, James O'Meara who had taken part in the hut tumbling came to own much of the property in Toomevara village by being 'in with an agent'. It was evident that he was 'in with' Donoghue as he played a significant role in the hut tumbling by telling the families in the huts to clear out on Donoghue's instructions and also spoke as a witness on Donoghue's behalf at the petty sessions case.[44] Another story which highlights the bitterness that was felt towards a family tells of how a member of the same family evicted a widow. She is said to have cursed them predicting that a time would come when they would not own any property in the parish. Whether this is true or a story which has been embellished by local people's bitterness or jealousy towards the family is unclear. Another saying which relates to two prominent families in the parish at this time is still known to some in the parish. 'If ever you feel you are near your doom, beware the Kennedys and Meaghers from Toome'. It was felt that these families were in positions of influence and 'in with the right people'. Bitterness felt towards Richard Wilson was unrelenting for many years. Eighty years after the clearances, he was openly regarded as the main villain behind the clearances. Regarded as a 'tyrannical' agent, he is remembered as wreaking 'havoc on the village of Toomevara. He reduced the village to one third of its size'.[45] Even to this day, while people may be cautious about openly discussing those who were involved in the tumbling of the huts, the name Wilson is still reviled.

Conclusion

This history of Toomevara during the Famine set out to describe the parish's experience between the years 1845 and 1851. Pre-Famine Toomevara was a fairly typical poor rural parish and quite similar to any of its surrounding parishes. For the most part, it suffered all the effects of the Famine one would expect in such a place. The overall population decreased by over 42%, meaning close to half of the parish's people perished or left the area. A similar effect was seen in housing in the parish with a corresponding decrease of 40% in inhabited houses. It is evident that it was mainly the poorer labouring class that were wiped out. High rates of emigration continued through the latter years of the Famine and long afterwards. Those who survived the Famine tended to have a somewhat-improved standard of living with higher average farm sizes and house values.

The severity of the clearances and the events that followed have continued to live in social memory in the area and this is indicative of the long-term bitterness engendered by what can partly be described as a class war at the time. In 1849, the clearance of the village was carried out by those with little regard for the welfare or survival of its inhabitants. News of the wholesale devastation that the clearance caused spread far and wide. The conditions in which those who remained in the village found themselves in are difficult to comprehend in the present day. Surviving in makeshift huts against the chapel walls was undoubtedly the height of deprivation and denigration, second only to starvation or the workhouse. However unfortunate this was, clearances such as this one in Toomevara were not unique. Clearances in other parts of the country such as Kilrush, Co. Clare, also reached the headlines causing much controversy. The events in Toomevara in February 1850 given the involvement of fellow parishioners in tumbling the shelter of those who were already impoverished, sparked a bitterness which remained in the social memory of the parish for generations.

The derogation of culpability for the suffering in Toomevara is not a clear cut case of blaming the lack of relief alone. As has been shown, there were numerous factors at play in Toomevara which caused much suffering. A large population, mainly made up of the poorer labouring class, dependence on the potato as a staple food, the high cost of alternative foods, the blight, the indifference of many who were in a position to help, incompetence and dishonesty on the part of some, the social network which provided security and survival for some and excluded others all played their own part. Overall,

Toomevara was set to experience the harsher effects of the Famine due to the precarious state of many of its inhabitants prior to 1845. As the tragic events unfolded, perhaps the saddest part of Toomevara's Famine history was the role some of its own people played in the suffering of their fellow parishioners.

Leabharlanna Poibli Chathair Bhaile Átha Cliath
Dublin City Public Libraries

Appendices

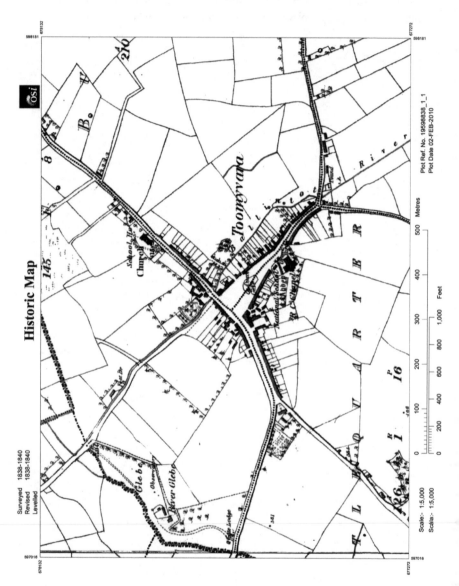

Appendix A: Toomevara 1840 (Copyright Permit No. MP 003310)

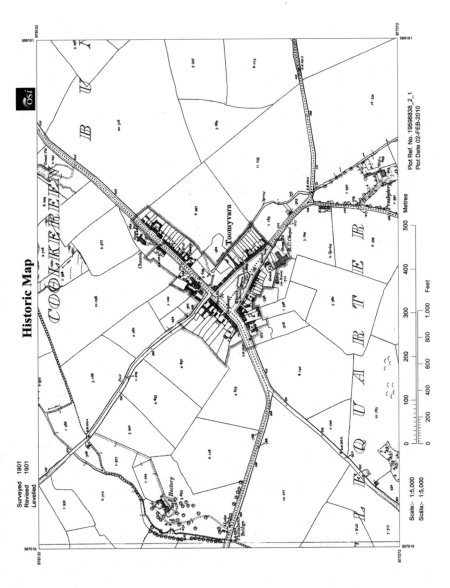

Appendix B: Toomevara 1901 (Copyright Permit No. MP 003310)

Notes

ABBREVIATIONS

IFC	Irish Folklore Commission
NAI	National Archives
NG	*Nenagh Guardian*
NLI	National Library of Ireland
NPLU	Nenagh poor law union
OS	Ordnance Survey
RABMD	Rental and account book Massy Dawson
RLFC	Famine Relief Commission Papers
THSJ	*Tipperary Historical Society Journal*
TM	Treacy memoirs
TV	*Tipperary Vindicator*

INTRODUCTION

1 Memoirs of Thomas Treacy of Toomevara, Co. Tipperary, 1832–1905 (MS in the possession of Ms Helena Kilmartin, Toomevara, Co. Tipperary). (hereafter TM)

2 *1851 census report*, pp 288–93, H.C. 1852–3 (1549), xci.649, 670–5; Roman Catholic parishes of Tipperary map (in possession of Tipperary local studies library, Thurles, County Tipperary).

3 Daniel Grace, *The great Famine in NPLU* (Nenagh, 2000), pp 181–4; Denis G. Marnane, 'The Famine in South Tipperary', pt 3 in *THSJ* (1998), 56–75.

4 *NG*, 6 Jun 1849.

5 M.E. Daly, *The Famine in Ireland* (Dublin, 1986); J.S. Donnelly Jnr, *The great Irish potato Famine* (2001); Melissa Fegan, *Literature and the Irish Famine* (Oxford, 2002); Cormac Ó Gráda, *Black 47 and beyond: the great Irish famine in history, economy and memory* (Princeton, 1999); Jacqueline Hill and Cormac Ó Gráda (eds), *The visitation of God? The potato and the great Irish Famine* (Dublin, 1993); Liam Kennedy, Paul S. Ell, E.M. Crawfod & L.A. Clarkson, *Mapping the great Irish Famine: a survey of the Famine decades* (Dublin, 1999); Christine Kinealy, *This great calamity, the Irish famine 1845–52* (Dublin, 1994); Christine Kinealy, *A death dealing famine, the great hunger in Ireland* (London, 1995); Noel Kissane, *The Irish Famine, a documentary history* (Dublin, 1995); Helen Litton, *The Irish Famine, an illustrated history* (Dublin, 1994); Cecil Woodham Smith, *The great hunger, Ireland 1845–1849* (London, 1961).

6 John Golby with Paul Smith, 'Oral sources' in M. Drake, R. Finnegan, J. Eustace (eds), *Studying family and community history 19th and 20th centuries volume 4. sources and methods: a handbook* (Cambridge, 1994), pp 103–7.

7 Ibid., p. 105.

8 Denis Marnane and Mary Guinan Darmody, *Finding Tipperary, a guide to the resources of the Tipperary studies department* (2007), p. 171.

9 Richard Griffith, *General valuation of rateable property in Ireland, 9 and 10 Vict. chapter 110. county of Tipperary, North Riding, barony of Upper Ormond* (Dublin, 1850) (hereafter Griffith's valuation)

10 Data taken from 1821, 1831 and 1841 census reports. *Abstract of the answers and returns made pursuant to an act of the united parliament, passed in the 55th year of the reign of His Late Majesty George the Third, intituled," an act to provide for taking an account of the population of Ireland, and for ascertaining the increase or diminution thereof." preliminary observations. Enumeration abstract. Appendix. M. DCCC. XXI*, pp 210–14, H.C. 1824 (577,1823), xxii.411, 644–8. (hereafter 1821 Census report); *Population, Ireland. Abstract of answers and returns under the population acts, 55 Geo. III. chap. 120. 3 Geo. IV. chap. 5. 2 Geo. IV. chap. 30. 1 Will. IV. chap. 19. Enumeration 1831*, p. 196, H.C. 1833 (634), xxxix.59, 256. (hereafter 1831 Census report); *Report of the commissioners appointed to take the census of*

Ireland, for the year 1841, p. 232, 256, H.C. 1843 (504), xxiv.1, 345, 368. (hereafter 1841 Census report); *The census of Ireland for the year 1851. part I. Showing the area, population, and number of houses, by townlands and electoral divisions. county of Tipperary. (North Riding.)*, pp 288–93, H.C. 1852–3 (1549), xci.649, 670–5. (hereafter 1851 Census report); Baptismal register of Toomevara Roman Catholic parish, Co. Tipperary, 1831–56 (Fr William McCormack, Toomevara, Co. Tipperary) (hereafter Toomevara R.C. baptismal register) Note: seven other baptisms were also registered but the dates of these are not discernible; Marriage register of Toomevara Roman Catholic parish, Co. Tipperary, 1831–56 (Fr William McCormack, Toomevara, Co. Tipperary) (hereafter Toomevara R.C. marriage register);

11 The Relief Commission (http://www.nationalarchives.ie/topics/famine/relief.html) (30 December 2008); 'Famine Relief Commission Papers, 1845–1847 database' (http://www.nationalarchives.ie/search/index.php?category=14) (30 December 2008).

12 Rental and account book of Massy Dawson estate of Toomevara, Co. Tipperary, 1840 (NAI, M 4471–8) (hereafter RABMD, 1840); Cole Bowen estate rental records, Ballymackey, Co. Tipperary, 1839–43 (Records in possession of Tipperary local studies, library Thurles, Co. Tipperary) (hereafter Cole Bowen estate rental records).

13 *Reports of commissioners for enquiring into the condition of the poorer classes in Ireland*, H.C. 1835–1836 (369), xxxii Pt. II.1.

1. TOOMEVARA BEFORE THE FAMINE

1 John Gleeson, *History of the Ely O'Carroll territory* (Dublin, 1915), pp 457–9.

2 E.H. Sheehan, *Nenagh and its neighbourhood* (3rd ed., Freshford, 1976), pp 48–9.

3 Samuel Lewis, *A topographical dictionary of Ireland. Comprising the several counties, cities, boroughs, corporate, market and post towns, parishes and villages with historical and statistical descriptions* (2 vols, London, 1837), ii, 638.

4 O.S. Map 6", Tipperary TY022 (1829–41). © Ordnance Survey Ireland / Government of Ireland, Copyright Permit No. MP 003310

5 Data taken from 1821, 1831 and 1841 census reports. *1821 Census report*, pp 210–214, H.C. 1824 (577,1823), xxii.411, 644–8; *1831 Census report*, p.196, H.C. 1833 (634), xxxix.59, 256.; *1841 Census report*, p. 232, 256, H.C. 1843 (504), xxiv.1, 345, 368.

6 Toomevara R.C. baptism register.

7 *1841 Census report*, p. 232, H.C. 1843 (504), xxiv.1, 345.

8 Ibid., p. 232, 256, H.C. 1843 (504), xxiv.1, 345, 368.

9 Grace, *NPLU*, p. 13.

10 *1841 Census report*, p. 232, H.C. 1843 (504), xxiv.1, 345.

11 *First report from His Majesty's commissioners for inquiring into the condition of the poorer classes in Ireland, with appendix A and supplement, supplement to appendix B, Pt. II*, p.223, H.C. 1835 (369), xxxii Pt.II.1, 745. (hereafter Poor Inquiry supplement to appendix B, part II).

12 *NG*, 31 July 1844.

13 *Poor Inquiry supplement to appendix B, part II*, p. 223, H.C. 1835 (369), xxxii Pt.II.1, 745.

14 Ibid., p. 223, H.C. 1835 (369), xxxii Pt.II.1, 745.

15 *1841 Census report*, p. xxxii, 223, H.C. 1843 (504), xxiv.1, 32, 345.

16 *TM*, p. 12.

17 *1821 Census report*, p. 211, H.C. 1824 (577,1823), xxii.411, 645; *Eighth report of the Commissioners of National Education in Ireland, for the year 1841*, H.C. 1842 [398], xxiii.339, pp 61–4. (hereafter National Education report 1841).

18 *National Education report 1841*, H.C. 1842 [398], xxiii.339, 61–4.

19 Grace, *NPLU*, p. 17.

20 William Hayes and Joseph Kennedy, *The parish churches of North Tipperary* (Tipperary, 2007), p. 95.

21 Hayes and Kennedy, *Parish churches of North Tipperary*, p. 91, p. 96.

22 *1841 Census report*, p. 233, H.C. 1843 (504), xxiv.1, 345.

23 *Devon commission part II*, p. 611, H.C. 1845 [616], xx.1, 611.

24 *NG*, 4 Jan. 1845.

25 *Devon commission part II*, p. 611, H.C. 1845 [616], xx.1, 611.

26 O.S. name book Tipperary; 1840; (NAI, OS88–5, p. 26); O.S. name book Tipperary; 1839; (NAI, OS88–20, p.13, p.15, p. 36); O.S. name book Tipperary; 1839; (NAI, OS88–141, p. 26); OS Map 6", Tipperary TY022 (1829–41); Grace, *NPLU*, p. 10.

27 *1841 Census report*, p. 233, H.C. 1843 (504), xxiv.1, 345; *TM*, p. 26.

28 *Returns of agricultural produce in Ireland, in the year 1847. Pt. II*, pp 12–3, H.C. 1847–8 [1000], lvii, 124–5.

29 *Devon commission part II*, p. 628, H.C. 1845 [616], xx.1, 634.

30 Ibid., p. 608, H.C. 1845 [616], xx.1, 614.

31 *Griffith's valuation*, pp 1–93.

32 Ibid., pp 1–11; 91–3.

33 Denis G. Marnane, 'A Tipperary landlord's diary of the 1860s' *THSJ*, 4 (1991), 121–8.

34 RABMD, 1840 (NAI, M4471–7); *Griffith's valuation*, pp 1–11; 91–3.

35 RABMD, 1833 (NAI, M4471–1); 1834 (NAI, M4471–2); 1836 (NAI, M4471–3); 1837 (NAI, M447148); 1838 (NAI, M4471–5); 1839 (NAI, M4471–6); 1840 (NAI, M4471–7); 1842 (NAI, M4471–8).

36 Cole Bowen estate rental records, 1839–43 (In possession of Tipperary local studies library.

37 *Devon commission part II*, pp 602–60, H.C. 1845 [616], xx.1, 608–66.

38 *Evidence taken before Her Majestys commissioners of inquiry into the state of the law and practice in respect to the occupation of land in Ireland. Pt. III*, p. 257, H.C. 1845 [657], xxx.1, 263 (hereafter Devon commission part III).

39 *Devon commission part II*, p. 614, H.C. 1845 [616], xx.1, 620.

40 Ibid., p. 608, H.C. 1845 [616], xx.1, 614; *Devon commission part III*, p. 254, H.C. 1845 [657], xxx.1, 259.

41 Grace, *NPLU*, p. 9.

42 *Devon commission part II*, pp 608–13, H.C. 1845 [616], xx.1, 614–19.

43 TM, p. 18; *TV*, 26 May 1849; NG, 20 May 1849.

44 *Devon commission part III*, p. 254–5, H.C. 1845 [657], xxx.1, 259–60.

45 Daniel Grace, 'Crime in pre-Famine North West Tipperary' in *THSJ*, 9 (1996), pp 84–95.

46 Ibid.

47 Noreen Higgins, *Tipperary's tithe war, 1830–1838* (2002), p. 217.

48 NG, 3 Aug. 1844–9 Aug. 1845.

49 NG, 19 Aug. 1844; 30 Oct. 1844; 18 Sept. 1844; 21 May 1845, 21 Dec. 1844.

50 For more on Terry Alts and other pre-Famine agrarian secret societies, see Stephen Gibbons, *Captain Rock, Night Errant: the threatening letters of pre-Famine Ireland* (Dublin,

2004) and Daniel Grace, 'The threatening notice in pre-Famine County Tipperary', *THSJ* (2009), 47–70.

51 *Devon commission part III*, pp 255–8, H.C. 1845 [657], xxx.1, 261–4.

52 *Devon commission part II*, p. 660, H.C. 1845 [616], xx.1, 666.

53 Ibid.

54 Patrick O'Donnell, *The Irish faction fighters of the nineteenth century* (Dublin, 1975), p. 9.

55 TM, p. 4.

56 Ibid., p. 5.

57 Ibid., p. 6.

58 Grace, *NPLU*, p. 3.

59 *Devon commission part II*, p.611, H.C. 1845 [616], xx.1, 611.

60 NG, 9 Apr. 1844; 21 Sept. 1844.

61 *TM*, p. 14.

2. FAMINE, 1845–9

1 NG, 25 Oct. 1845; 22 Oct. 1845.

2 Kinealy, *A death dealing Famine*, p. 59.

3 Grace, *NPLU*, p. 42.

4 Ó Gráda, *Black '47 and beyond*, p. 38.

5 *TM*, p. 19.

6 Kinealy, *A death dealing Famine*, p. 62.

7 Donnelly, *The great Irish potato Famine*, p. 54.

8 Grace, *NPLU*, p. 54.

9 Ibid., p. 55.

10 *1851 census report*, pp 288–93, H.C. 1852–3 (1549), xci.649, 670–5.

11 Grace, *NPLU*, p. 54.

12 Grace, *NPLU*, p. 59.

13 Ibid., p. 63.

14 RLFC3/2/27/ 120; NG, 28 Apr. 1846.

15 *Griffith's valuation*, pp 16–27.

16 RLFC3/2/27/ 120; Smithwick family, Tipperary (http://www.smithwickfamily.org/tipperary/paf/pafg08.htm#227) (29 Aug. 2009); Smithwick family history (http://users.tpg.com.au/users/graemeb/tree.htm) (29 Aug. 2009).

17 RLFC3/2/27/ 120.

18 NG, 28 Apr. 1846; *Griffith's valuation*, pp 1–93.

19 RLFC3/2/27/ 120.

20 *Griffith's valuation*, pp 18–21.

21 RLFC3/2/27/ 120.

22 RLFC6/27/50, 54, 55; Grace, *NPLU*, p. 62.

23 RLFC6/27/54; Grace, *NPLU*, pp 66–8.

24 Grace, *NPLU*, p. 75.

25 RLFC6/27/54.

26 RLFC3/1/2069.

27 Donnelly, *The great Irish potato Famine*, p. 54.

28 RLFC6/27/54.

29 Donnelly, *The great Irish potato Famine*, p. 55.

30 RLFC3/1/4799; RLFC3/1/4508.

31 Kinealy, *A death dealing Famine*, p. 63.

32 Ibid., p. 72.

33 RLFC/4/27/173, 176, 180, 18

34 Donnelly, *The great Irish potato Famine*, p. 58.

35 Ibid., p. 57; RLFC5/27/01.

36 RLFC3/2/27/128.

37 NG, 30 Aug. 1848; 14 Oct. 1846.

38 RLFC3/2/27/ 121.

39 NG, 14 Oct. 1846.

40 Grace, *NPLU*, p. 50.

41 RLFC3/2/27/128.

42 NG, 16 May 1846; 15 Mar. 1848.

43 Ibid., 30 Sept. 1846; Donnelly, *The great Irish potato Famine*, p. 72.

44 NG, 16 Sept. 1846; 14 Oct. 184

45 *TV*, 23 Jan. 1847; NG, 27 Jan. 1847.

46 NG, 27 Jan. 1847.

47 Ibid., 2 May 1846; 10 June 1846; 17 June 1846; 29 July 1846; 26 Sept. 1846 NG, 3 Oc 1846.

48 Daly, *Famine in Ireland*, p. 57.

49 Kinealy, *A death dealing Famine* p. 79.

50 NG, 17 Oct. 1846; *Relief of distress 1847*, p. 247, H.C. 1847 [797], lii.1, 25.

51 Kinealy, *A death dealing Famine* p. 123.

52 NG, 12 Jan. 1847.